Number 107
Fall 2005

New Directions for Evaluation

Jean A. King
Editor-in-Chief

D1569468

Social Network Analysis in Program Evaluation

Maryann M. Durland
Kimberly A. Fredericks
Editors

SOCIAL NETWORK ANALYSIS IN PROGRAM EVALUATION
Maryann M. Durland, Kimberly A. Fredericks (eds.)
New Directions for Evaluation, no. 107
Jean A. King, Editor-in-Chief

Microfilm copies of issues and articles are available in 16mm and 35mm, as well as microfiche in 105mm, through University Microfilms Inc., 300 North Zeeb Road, Ann Arbor, Michigan 48106-1346.

New Directions for Evaluation is indexed in Contents Pages in Education, Higher Education Abstracts, and Sociological Abstracts.

NEW DIRECTIONS FOR EVALUATION (ISSN 1097-6736, electronic ISSN 1534-875X) is part of The Jossey-Bass Education Series and is published quarterly by Wiley Subscription Services, Inc., a Wiley company, at Jossey-Bass, 989 Market Street, San Francisco, California 94103-1741.

SUBSCRIPTIONS cost $80.00 for U.S./Canada/Mexico; $104 international. For institutions, agencies, and libraries, $185 U.S.; $225 Canada; $259 international. Prices subject to change.

EDITORIAL CORRESPONDENCE should be addressed to the Editor-in-Chief, Jean A. King, University of Minnesota, 330 Wulling Hall, 86 Pleasant Street SE, Minneapolis, MN 55455.

www.josseybass.com

Editorial Policy and Procedures

New Directions for Evaluation, a quarterly sourcebook, is an official publication of the American Evaluation Association. The journal publishes empirical, methodological, and theoretical works on all aspects of evaluation. A reflective approach to evaluation is an essential strand to be woven through every volume. The editors encourage volumes that have one of three foci: (1) craft volumes that present approaches, methods, or techniques that can be applied in evaluation practice, such as the use of templates, case studies, or survey research; (2) professional issue volumes that present issues of import for the field of evaluation, such as utilization of evaluation or locus of evaluation capacity; (3) societal issue volumes that draw out the implications of intellectual, social, or cultural developments for the field of evaluation, such as the women's movement, communitarianism, or multiculturalism. A wide range of substantive domains is appropriate for *New Directions for Evaluation;* however, the domains must be of interest to a large audience within the field of evaluation. We encourage a diversity of perspectives and experiences within each volume, as well as creative bridges between evaluation and other sectors of our collective lives.

The editors do not consider or publish unsolicited single manuscripts. Each issue of the journal is devoted to a single topic, with contributions solicited, organized, reviewed, and edited by a guest editor. Issues may take any of several forms, such as a series of related chapters, a debate, or a long article followed by brief critical commentaries. In all cases, the proposals must follow a specific format, which can be obtained from the editor-in-chief. These proposals are sent to members of the editorial board and to relevant substantive experts for peer review. The process may result in acceptance, a recommendation to revise and resubmit, or rejection. However, the editors are committed to working constructively with potential guest editors to help them develop acceptable proposals.

Jean A. King, Editor-in-Chief
University of Minnesota
330 Wulling Hall
86 Pleasant Street SE
Minneapolis, MN 55455
e-mail: kingx004@umn.edu

CONTENTS

EDITORS' NOTES

This volume of *New Directions for Evaluation*, devoted to applications and discussion of data collection and analysis methodology, introduces social network analysis (SNA) and its application to evaluation practice. The chapter authors briefly describe the methodology, provide an overview of the measures that comprise some of a social network analyst's tools, and illustrate the application of the method to four evaluation case studies. The final chapters include a personal account of current SNA use by a government agency and suggestions for future use of SNA for evaluation practice.

SNA has a long and complex history that we barely touch on in this volume. Our intent is to provide an introduction to the methodology that might pique the curiosity of a variety of readers. Network analysis methodology can be extremely quantitative and technical. One of the criticisms of the field of SNA is that the bulk of the work is academic and does not bring forth simple or practical applications. Few texts within the field of network analysis provide both an understanding of the concept and directions and processes for clear application of the methodology. There are currently no known books that specifically apply network analysis to program evaluation.

We believe that this volume can help bridge the gap between the development of a methodology and its use within a specific discipline such as program evaluation. SNA is based on a way of viewing evaluation through the lens of relationships, compared to traditional methodologies that can be categorized as attribute focused. The application of SNA is not determined by the context of the evaluation or by the subject area or field, such as whether the evaluation is formative or summative, value free, utilization focused, in-house or external, in the area of education reform, about online collaborations, or a measure of the quality of management. The use of SNA is determined by questions about the nature of the relationships of the networks relative to a specific project, program, or initiative, whether that relationship is between people, organizations, events, or ideas. SNA can provide evaluators with tools for identifying and exploring the structures that form or are formed by networks, whether they are formal or informal, static or changing. The emphasis in this volume is on highlighting the conceptual framework and differentiating SNA from traditional methods.

The listing of the editors in this volume is alphabetical and represents equal contributions by both.

NEW DIRECTIONS FOR EVALUATION, no. 107, Fall 2005   © Wiley Periodicals, Inc.
Published online in Wiley InterScience (www.interscience.wiley.com) • DOI: 10.1002/ev.156

1

Because this is an introduction for the field of program evaluation, we are writing for a broad range of readers. The volume will be differentially applicable for four levels of practitioners. First are evaluators who want to increase their understanding of SNA and the processes and procedures for using the methodology to answer specific evaluation questions. We provide enough details of the measures that are illustrated in the case studies to provide this level of practitioner with a conceptual framework and procedural steps for including SNA within an evaluation project. We do not, however, intend this volume to be a practical manual for use but rather a step forward in clarifying the conceptual framework for SNA, which is different from traditional methodologies, and then to open the discussion for taking the next steps. To implement SNA within an evaluation design, the evaluator would need further skills to develop questions appropriate for the data, to be able to align SNA measures to evaluation questions based on the theoretical framework of the evaluation study and the measure, and to be proficient at using one of the software packages available for SNA or at creating the necessary algorithms with other statistical packages.

The second group of practitioners consists of evaluators who are interested in understanding more about the choice of questions appropriate for SNA and the alignment of a question to a specific measure. As we and the chapter authors explore the methodology further in Chapter Three and in the case studies, practitioners can see how SNA questions provide a different view of evaluation and how this view relates to more traditional evaluation questions.

The third set of practitioners comprises those who might want to explore connections between an SNA conceptual framework and other theoretical frameworks, such as systems perspectives and complexity and communication and other networks that may define an evaluation project. These areas are touched on in Chapter Three's exploration of the methodology, and in the final chapter's discussion of the potential for future applicability in evaluation practice.

In the fourth group are practitioners who want a broader view of a methodology but are not currently interested in pursuing any specific applications. We have written this volume so that evaluation practitioners can explore the methodology without feeling they are reading a textbook. We acknowledge that this volume is metaphorically the tip of the iceberg in the applications of SNA to evaluation practice.

We begin by clarifying and defining terms, setting the parameters of evaluation practice that we are addressing, and discussing what determines a methodology. Chapter Two briefly reviews the history and development of SNA. SNA is not a new methodology, and glimpsing its historical roots provides a clue as to its complexity, its theoretical foundations, and the current interest in its applications.

Chapter Three illustrates and explores the most common measures used in SNA. Here Maryann Durland presents two themes. First, in the application of SNA for evaluation purposes, the choice of a measure is aligned with the theory of the relationship under study. Understanding the basic structure of the measures and the levels of analysis provides a framework for an evaluator to determine whether a measure is appropriate for a particular evaluation question. Second, many of the algorithms and analysis tools in SNA are also used in traditional methods of data analysis. Durland highlights in Chapter Three that although the mathematics and statistics are similar, the interpretations are conceptually different. Chapter Three is not meant to be a manual for immediate application, but rather a framework for understanding the concepts and language of SNA, and it will guide the evaluator through the overall language and conceptual framework in reading the case studies that follow.

The next four chapters are case studies that illustrate how SNA was used to answer specific evaluation questions. The authors of the fourth chapter, Susan Kochan and Charles Teddlie, used SNA in an early evaluation of the communication patterns in a high school study as part of a larger evaluation. Their chapter provides examples of two important points: how SNA can fit into an evaluation design and how the technology and the methodology of doing SNA have advanced and improved over the processes of mapping a network by hand. When this evaluation was first conducted, the tools for doing SNA were not readily available to researchers or evaluators. Most of the computer tools were complex and mainframe based, so individuals familiar with the methods created maps by hand and calculated the measures with mainframe programs. This chapter clarifies the differences between hand-drawn maps and those calculated by algorithms. The purpose of maps, as illustrations of calculations, and the alignment of maps to the measures are topics of an ongoing conversation within the SNA community.

Chapter Five offers the network analysis of a program for the developmentally disabled. Kimberly Fredericks presents the findings from the network analysis of a demonstration program and compares them with the findings of a comprehensive program evaluation. This case analysis was conducted by interviewing key stakeholders at evaluation implementation sites across one state. The chapter illustrates how SNA was used with analysis of networks of key actors to understand an evaluation question. It shows the complexity of decision making and how multiple ways of viewing help to clarify the parameters of the decision and guide decision-making processes.

In Chapter Six, Sandra Birk shares an example of using SNA to answer one complex evaluation question with forty-seven individual networks. It is an instance of a highly specific evaluation focus, the evaluation of capacity, defined as the ability to conduct the next generation of research. In this context, *capacity* refers to the individuals who have specific knowledge in any of the critical areas. This evaluation reveals how the patterns of networks illustrate differential levels of capacity, demonstrating how findings are often supportive of intuitive information that has not been previously identified and how SNA can provide formative information. One result from the evaluation was as simple as a manager realizing it was necessary to go back and meet individuals on work teams who had been identified by others as important.

Chapter Seven, by Maryann Durland, is an evaluation of the integration of two large departments. The merger was an initiative planned to increase capacity and efficiency. The integration had been well planned, included moving individuals around from one of four locations, and all of the participants had had extensive preparation, training, and time to meet prior to the integration. The evaluation was conducted to examine the extent to which the two departments were integrated and working on common projects.

We end with visions and suggestions for the future. Chapter Eight, by David Introcaso, is a reaction to and summary of a current application of SNA to evaluation practice. Chapter Nine presents our views on the potential of the methodology for application in evaluation practice. We hope our discussion in this chapter will open the way for further conversation on the methodology, its application to evaluation practice, and the next steps for evaluation.

It is our intention that this volume be both informative and spark a new area of interest for evaluators. We look forward to further discussions, debates, and sharing of application details about SNA with other evaluation practitioners.

Maryann M. Durland
Kimberly A. Fredericks
Editors

MARYANN M. DURLAND is an independent consultant specializing in evaluation and the applications of social network analysis.

KIMBERLY M. FREDERICKS is assistant professor of public administration and policy in the Department of Political Science, Indiana State University.

1

The application of social network analysis methodologies is relatively new for mainstream evaluation and has yet to be fully explored in this discipline. This chapter discusses how and why SNA is appropriate for evaluation practice.

An Introduction to Social Network Analysis

Maryann M. Durland, Kimberly A. Fredericks

This volume explores the use and integration of social network analysis (SNA) methodology into evaluation practice. This volume is not meant to be an all-encompassing manual for doing SNA. Our goal is rather to point out the key characteristics of the methodology and its applications and to suggest the potential fit between the methodology and particular questions that may be components of an evaluation design.

The application of SNA methodology to social science research has steadily increased over the past ten to fifteen years. Three factors have led to this increased interest in and use of SNA. First, practical applications have conceptualized new understandings of interactions. When the magazine *Business 2.0* featured an SNA article on terrorist networks in December 2001 (Stewart, 2001), interest was piqued. Developing online networks is an important tool for online businesses, so when $7 million in venture capital was poured into Friendster, an online networking tool for individuals to create and explore their personal and business networks interactively, interest grew. One business model mines these networks to sell as data back to participating businesses to increase sales.

Even in the environment of unclear regulations and network ownership, creating, visualizing, and tapping into personal and business networks are activities that are seeing increased use. University students can find classmates and friends and keep in touch with others, with firewalled and university-supported online products such as www.thefacebook.com, where students can create their own online communities, find friends, and even

NEW DIRECTIONS FOR EVALUATION, no. 107, Fall 2005   © Wiley Periodicals, Inc.
Published online in Wiley InterScience (www.interscience.wiley.com) • DOI: 10.1002/ev.157

search for other students, such as those taking the same classes, by picture. However, although this level of social networks is what people may notice, it is not the same as the application of SNA to relational data. The algorithms and technology may be similar to those of an analyst, but these applications are used to create visual representations for conceptualization, not for the analysis of the networks. At this level, there are common points for the application of the technology underneath both building networks and doing SNA.

At a level of practical application and analysis more aligned to evaluation goals, we know that SNA is important, as companies like IBM, Accenture, and Mars are using it internally or with clients to determine which individuals work together or consult on projects, who holds influence, and who needs to meet whom. In other words, SNA is important because corporate America has seen the potential for its use in improving organizational effectiveness (Cross and Parker, 2004).

A second factor for the increased interest in the application of SNA, particularly at the corporate and business level, is its development and focus on understanding complexity and systems. A system at its most basic level can be defined as a set of components with at least one relation between the components. At a broader level, a system is a group of interacting, interrelated, or interdependent elements forming a complex whole. Structural properties of networks are systemic elements and the interactions of structural elements, such as found in informal communication patterns, work group interactions, and leadership paths, which are features for understanding complexity and system properties.

The history of the development of formal evaluation activities has been explored for many years. Systems thinking, the complexity and interactional nature of organizational structures, and the strategies for implementing, describing, and understanding complex initiatives are all current topics in evaluation discussion, problem resolution, and program theory development. In line with these evolving theoretical constructs, evaluation designs also have to reflect how we interpret and understand complexity, systems, systemic change, and structure, and SNA is a methodology for doing that.

The third factor for the increased interest in networks, which underlies all other indicators of SNA growth, has been the availability of software programs that facilitate the analysis of data and the creation of sociograms. SNA has a history beginning in the early 1930s across many disciplines, including anthropology, economics, transportation planning, and business. The methodology has had a somewhat consistent use as a research tool, but even across these disciplines, interest in and use of the methodology has increased recently, due mostly to technological advances for data analysis. Although most programs are difficult for the average user, as they were developed for personal or limited distribution by mathematicians, sociologists, graph theorists, and information technology specialists, many of these programs are now posted for distribution and exploration by evaluators.

Overall, SNA applications have reached into such diverse areas as identifying knowledge leaders in organizations, measuring collaboration on teams, illustrating the hidden patterns of terrorism, planning transportation networks, and exploring the paths of disease in public health. Many sociology and business departments teach classes or have complete fields of study in SNA, and an increasing number of doctoral dissertations across a variety of disciplines use the methodology. However, the application of SNA methodology to mainstream program evaluation is relatively new. It was not until 1998 that network analysis as a methodology appeared in the American Evaluation Association conference program.

In this chapter, the volume editors explore the evaluation landscape that we believe provides many appropriate opportunities for the application of SNA. We explain and explore SNA so that readers can make judgments about the applicability of SNA to their own work and whether to pursue the methodology. Our goal is to provide evaluators a framework for determining if there is a fit between the evaluation questions that they have and the potential for this methodology to answer those questions.

Methodology

There are as many unique applications of evaluation as there are combinations of evaluation models and theories, program theories, disciplines, service areas, analysis techniques and methods, and client needs. In the process of creating a design for an evaluation, evaluators establish questions and indicators that form a framework for multiple areas and levels of decision making. One of those areas is methodology.

Whether evaluators follow a particular evaluation model or theoretical perspective, in evaluation design we make decisions about the data, including what are considered data, what to collect, how to collect them, and at what level the data will be aggregated for analysis and reporting. Evaluators make decisions about what kinds of data are appropriate for answering a specific question, if the data are aligned to program goals and objectives, and how best to answer specific questions.

For example, if evaluators want to know whether a program is reaching its goal of increasing the diversity of participants who take part in its activities, we might collect demographic data on participants and analyze these data quantitatively and, if possible and applicable, compare them to past data. We would most likely present the results of the data in a table or chart with descriptive statistics and, if the design allowed, inferential statistics. If our questions focused more on whether stakeholder perceptions encourage diverse populations to participate in a program's activities and events, then we might decide that qualitative interviews would be the best method for answering this question, and our results might be a summary of the main points stakeholders brought up in conversation.

Decisions about the design of an evaluation reflect both the characteristics and dynamics of a program and the appropriateness and usefulness of methods, strategies, and tools an evaluator selects. Evaluators typically study actors, activities, or events, such as students who attend a program or receive services, mentors who receive training, organizations that restructure, team effectiveness, programs that provide services, the participants in an initiative, and so on. Evaluation is about determining the degree of impact or the amount and characteristics of program effect on or because of the actors, activities, or events.

Traditional methodologies concentrate on what many call attribute analysis (Knoke and Kuklinski, 1982; Laumann, Marsden, and Prensky, 1989; Wellman, 1988). The major characteristic of attribute analysis is that the unit of analysis is the individual, and the variable or element under evaluation is the trait or behavior of that individual, which could be a person, organization, event, or something else (Freeman, 1989; Rogers and Kincaid, 1981).

The data that evaluators collect on a trait or behavior can be called *elements, variables,* or *attributes.* Evaluators collect data on a variable with a measure or an instrument and through data analysis determine some indication of the value of something. In evaluation designs, one of the critical tasks that evaluators undertake is to separate the kinds of information that are the outcomes related to program tasks and activities (such as the number of individuals served, tested, or treated; workshops offered; performance; home visits; days in rehabilitation; or activities completed) and information related to the program components that lead to the outcomes (such as processes, characteristics, resources, activities, and structures). From a design standpoint, evaluators develop and find measures that will indicate where and how in the program components the value of a program exists, as well as to determine whether an outcome occurred and the extent to which it occurred.

Evaluation practice is not just about making judgments about value, but about how the judgments of value are determined. Evaluators look for the indicators, causal paths, and places and incidents that can be measured in some manner. The measures provide the indications that the program and its implementation may be in some way causally linked to the outcomes. For example, an evaluator in a large urban area is designing an evaluation for a mentoring program created to address the needs of twelve-year-olds who are not yet involved in gang activities. The overall outcome of the program is preventing future gang involvement. The mentoring program includes training for mentors on specific mentoring, program activities, and recruitment strategies for engaging twelve-year-olds. In the evaluation design, one evaluation path may be to determine if the training was sufficient for the mentors to carry out the activities as planned, if the activities were appropriate for the population of clients served, and if the children recruited were those who would benefit from the program. Evaluators might be interested in determining how well the training prepared mentors for their role in activities and then the impact of the activities on twelve-year-olds' future gang activities. Or they might explore the recruitment process or whether the mentoring program provided sufficient support and tools for twelve-year-olds to rebuff gang activity and allegiance.

Evaluators want to be clear that a program's intentions and implementation can be measured and that the value of the components can be linked to understanding the outcomes that are anticipated. Did fewer twelve-year-olds in fact end up in gangs or exhibit associated gang-related behavior?

Evaluators outline program components and processes in tools such as logic models, where the connections from program activities to outcomes are defined and explained (McLaughlin and Jordan, 2004). These tools help evaluators identify where to look for information, the kinds of questions to ask, and the important components to explore. Across disciplines, evaluators use traditional methodologies, both qualitative and quantitative, to sort, enumerate, describe, and explain these elements or variables in their evaluation work to obtain indicators of program merit or worth.

Traditional methodologies have two key assumptions: (1) there is an independence between the components of a program, and (2) there is a differential or correlational nature of explanation. In other words, we evaluate programs under the assumption that the attitudes, characteristics, or behavior of one item are not influenced by any other studied. What is important are the differences in the attitudes, characteristics, or behaviors of each item or the relation of the variables studied to other characteristics (Wasserman and Faust, 1994). These two assumptions form the basic premise for developing designs to answer evaluation questions.

SNA is the study of relationships within the context of social situations. It contains the set of measures and analysis tools that are used to describe and understand relational data. Relational data indicate whether a relationship between two components or actors exists and the value of that relationship. Social network theory stands apart from other methodological theories as it focuses on the social context and behavior of relationships among actors (that is, subjects or objects under investigation) rather than on the rational choices individual actors make. This is the basic assumption that differentiates SNA from other evaluation methods.

Another difference in methodology is that other methods result in an understanding of importance or the significance of the differences or correlations. The results for SNA are more complex, and the importance or significance of findings can rarely be determined with one statistic. SNA is a view into the complexity of programs that often begins with a small question that, like a funnel, opens up into something much bigger. That does not mean that SNA is a never-ending journey into analysis, but rather that it provides many more clues into the function of programs.

For example, in the mentoring program with twelve-year-olds, an important characteristic of the program is that mentors encourage and support the children in developing new friendships within the group. One network measure would be to ask the children to name their best friends and those they hang out with at the start of the program and at intervals during the program. Changes in the children's networks to include more friendships within the group and fewer with friends on the street would indicate that the program was having the desired effect. This measure would result in an egonet for each child. An *egonet* is all of the connections to and from one person and could include the connections between those connections (indirect connections to the ego). Another measure, captured from the same data, might be the network of the group and measures of internal connections versus external connections. An analysis of these data would reveal if any members of the group were becoming leaders, if there were members who still had or were developing more external gang-related friends, and if those members had any direct or indirect influence on the group. We would have both numerical data and sociograms to explore. Sociograms illustrate the relationships being measured or that can be constructed from the data resulting from an analysis. They are powerful tools for understanding how the results of the data analysis coincide with the pattern of connections. In the cases presented in this volume, the chapter authors have primarily used sociograms to illustrate the results of the data analysis, though some numerical data are also provided.

The premise for traditional methods is that evaluators select measures and instruments through the evaluation design that will inform defined questions. They make assumptions that they have asked the right questions, have gathered the best data to answer those questions, and from the results make determinations of value. Going further, they may also make recommendations in evaluation reports based on information from the evaluation design, processes, and data analysis or on conclusions made. These premises are applicable to SNA as well.

Application to Program Evaluation

Like most other innovations in their early stages, SNA has yet to be fully explored. This volume initiates a conversation about the fit of SNA to the practice of program evaluation. A primary function of the choice of a methodology is that it should suit the questions that it is used to inform. Interest in SNA has grown as the potential for the tools to answer more complex structural questions is put into practice and as the tools themselves have become more user friendly.

SNA is not an organizational outline, a logic model of relationships, a conceptual framework, or a relational database. There are other tools, such as concept mapping, that have the appearance of SNA and are structurally and methodologically similar but are purposively and conceptually different. Both SNA and concept mapping, as used by Trochim, are theoretically about connections, and both can use algorithms such as multidimensional scaling to determine clusters, but they are different methods for different purposes. Trochim (1989) and Jackson and Trochim (2002) describe concept mapping as a structured six-step process that takes qualitative and quantitative data from participants to produce a pictorial view (concept map) of the targeted ideas and concepts and how these are interrelated and valued. SNA takes relational data that form a network, generally dichotomous, and analyzes these data with a variety of measures. Concept mapping uses both qualitative and quantitative data with gap analysis and clustering to create a complex map of a particular conceptual framework. It is a method with specific procedures for calculations and products. SNA, though conceptually simple, analyzes data in a matrix format, is more of a theoretical framework that includes decision points such as the choice of measures and the level of the relationship, and provides insight into what that relationship means and how it is structured.

As evaluators have begun to describe and understand the complexity of organizations better, we have been looking for tools to help both describe organizations and their programs and make sense of, understand, and evaluate their components. As organizations develop and implement more complex programs in response to their own increased understandings about complexity and systemic change and as evaluators develop evaluation designs from program goals and objectives that reflect that complexity, we also need to adopt methodologies to measure and understand that complexity.

For example, in our evaluation design of work teams or communities of practice, evaluators might have asked questions about who was involved in the planning for the teams or collaborations or about the content of communication. We might have ended up with a comprehensive list of people, categorized by departments, grade levels, or the roles that they played in implementing the project. With traditional methodologies, the data would have been descriptive. Another kind of data to collect would be the content of meetings that people attended and a qualitative analysis of those data. Each of these methods provides a linear view of a program and the organization implementing the program. These views are like sticking straws into a program and viewing the program through them. No matter how long the straw or how many are used, each view is unique, linear, and separate from the others. You can control the depth to which you go into the program, but each straw can go only so far.

SNA is a methodology for understanding the capacity of an organization to engage in its activities based on its organization structure, operationally defined or not, both informally and formally. It helps to get at the structure of an organization beyond the linear additive elements of program components. With SNA, the whole is greater than the sum of its parts. Understanding and identifying the parts within the context of the whole provides a degree of information that gets at the issues of complexity and system dynamics. For example, taking the earlier scenario, SNA would provide a snapshot of each work team and the structure of communication patterns within those teams based on a particular question. SNA data are often collected through a survey, and a question appropriate to this scenario might be, "With whom do you primarily work to achieve the goals of your team?" Knowing that each team is meeting once a week is linear data; knowing that there are two cliques in team B and that there is no communication between them is structural and provides data that can be acted on. The structure of this team provides an indication of its capacity to engage in collaborative activities that are designed to achieve defined goals. The application of SNA appears particularly appropriate to several types of evaluation practice, for example, the evaluation of collaboration and communities of practice and participatory evaluation. The feedback from SNA can be a critical source of information on what works within a program.

Theoretically and practically, when programs define their activities and how implementation will take place, they use terms and indicators of structure: "our mission," "working together," "in collaboration," "forming work teams," and so on. These structural features define the framework for implementation strategies, and as evaluators we often assume that by defining the structure, the structure therefore exists. Complexity and systems thinking help us to understand that this is naive. Structure indicates a capacity of an organization to engage in the activities it chooses to attain its goals. Capacity is not a linear activity in itself to be implemented. Underneath the success of the programs we evaluate is the capacity of an organization to implement the structural strategies and features that are either explicitly or implicitly defined. Thus, fully understanding program structure and process requires looking at the dynamic nature of the organization.

Although the editors and authors of this volume only touch the surface of SNA, the Additional Resources section at the end of the volume provides interested readers with a list of key readings, software programs, and Web sites for further study. In addition, each chapter has references that will guide readers to other resources on specific topics.

References

Cross, R., and Parker, A. *The Hidden Power of Social Networks: Understanding How Work Really Gets Done in Organizations.* Boston: Harvard Business School Press, 2004.

Freeman, L. C. "Social Networks and the Structure Experiment." In L. C. Freeman, D. R. White, and A. K. Romney (eds.), *Research Methods in Social Network Analysis.* Fairfax, Va.: George Mason University Press, 1989.

Jackson, K., and Trochim, W. "Concept Mapping as an Alternative Approach for the Analysis of Open-Ended Survey Responses." *Organizational Research Methods,* 2002, 5(4), 307–336.

Knoke, D., and Kuklinski, J. H. *Network Analysis.* Thousand Oaks, Calif.: Sage, 1982.

Laumann, E. O., Marsden, P. V., and Prensky, D. "The Boundary Specification Problem in Network Analysis." In L. C. Freeman, D. R. White, and A. K. Romney (eds.),

Research Methods in Social Network Analysis. Fairfax, Va.: George Mason University Press, 1989.

McLaughlin, J., and Jordan, G. "Using Logic Models." In J. Wholey, H. Hatry, and K. Newcomer (eds.), *Handbook of Practical Program Evaluation.* (2nd ed.) San Francisco: Jossey-Bass, 2004.

Rogers, E. M., and Kincaid, D. L. *Communication Networks: Toward a New Paradigm for Research.* New York: Macmillan, 1981.

Stewart, T. A. "Six Degrees of Mohamed Atta." *Business 2.0,* December 2001.

Trochim, W. "An Introduction to Concept Mapping for Planning and Evaluation." *Evaluation and Program Planning,* 1989, *12,* 1–16.

Wasserman, S., and Faust, K. *Social Network Analysis: Methods and Applications.* Cambridge: Cambridge University Press, 1994.

Wellman, B. "Structural Analysis: From Method and Metaphor to Theory and Substance." In B. Wellman and S. D. Berkowitz (eds.), *Social Structures: A Network Approach.* Cambridge: Cambridge University Press, 1988.

MARYANN M. DURLAND is an independent consultant specializing in evaluation and in the applications of social network analysis.

KIMBERLY A. FREDERICKS is assistant professor of public administration and policy in the Department of Political Science, Indiana State University.

2

This chapter provides a brief history of the development of network analysis, an overview of the methodology, and an exploration of its key concepts.

The Historical Evolution and Basic Concepts of Social Network Analysis

Kimberly A. Fredericks, Maryann M. Durland

Social network theory stands apart from other social science theory because it focuses on the social context and behavior of relationships between actors rather than on the rational choices individual actors make, as seen in disciplines such as economics and the social and decision sciences. Traditional social sciences do not consider the existence of these social aspects of relationships as data. Even organizational sociology, which one might consider a more socially oriented field, disregards social ties and primarily studies individual characteristics of groups (Kilduff and Tsai, 2003).

Social network analysis (SNA) applications have had three main and parallel influences beginning in the 1930s. The first was sociometric analysis, which used graph theory methods. The second was a mathematical approach taken up first by Kurt Lewin and later by Harvard researchers, which laid the foundation for the analysis of social networks. The Harvard analysis introduced the notion of cliques, which operationalized social structures. No longer was network analysis merely descriptive in nature. The third influence came from the Manchester anthropologists who looked at the structure of community relations in villages. All traditions were brought together, again at Harvard, in the 1960s and 1970s when contemporary SNA was developed (Kilduff and Tsai, 2003).

Both the identification and the analysis of the structure of relationships within groups have been the subject of inquiry since the early 1930s. In the 1930s, German Gestalt theorists in psychology came to the United States to work. The most notable was Jacob Moreno (1934), who investigated how

New Directions for Evaluation, no. 107, Fall 2005 © Wiley Periodicals, Inc.
Published online in Wiley InterScience (www.interscience.wiley.com) • DOI: 10.1002/ev.158

an individual's group relations affected his or her actions and hence his or her psychological development. Moreno was credited with devising the sociogram as a way to depict such social relationships. The sociogram is a diagram in the tradition of spatial geometry, with individuals represented as points (nodes) and relationships being the lines connecting individuals' points. The sociogram provides a visual representation of the social structure under investigation and illuminates particular aspects of the relationships that constitute the structure. For example, the relationship lines in the sociogram could represent resource or communication flows or influence, or could provide an illustration of the connections among individuals. Most research at the time focused on the relationships of small groups of two or three individuals, known, respectively, as dyads or triads (Scott, 2000).

In the 1950s, Dorwin Cartwright and Frank Harary built on Moreno's work and connected the sociogram to mathematical formulas to create graph theory. In early graph theory, lines began to have value, either positive or negative, reflecting the direction of a relationship or influence. They also began to include arrowheads at the end to denote relationship direction or flow. This allowed the analysis of group structure from the standpoint of each individual concurrently, creating the notion of asymmetry and balance in network theory and analysis (Kilduff and Tsai, 2003).

Between 1927 and 1932 the famous Hawthorne studies were conducted by Elton Mayo and other researchers, who used sociograms to map informal social structures and group behavior in a bank's wiring room (Scott, 2000). This was the first major study that used sociograms to depict and analyze social relations. In 1941, W. Lloyd Warner and Paul Lunt studied a small urban community in New England that was found to have many intimate circles among its inhabitants. From this work, the term *clique* was born in mainstream sociology and network theory. Warner and Lunt described the notion that overlapping and interrelating cliques construct a social system. The New England town they studied was largely connected by a vast subsystem of informal ties (Scott, 2000). From this, a network language was devised. Moving beyond language, Radcliffe-Browne was one of the first to conceptualize structure and suggest the need for a separate theoretical and methodological "branch of natural science" (Radcliffe-Browne, 1959, p. 190) for exploring social structure.

Most of the work of the mathematicians and the graph theorists was based on complicated and complex algorithms. Applications were difficult and slow and usually done on small groups because of the complexity and time-consuming nature of the calculations. Creating one small sociogram by hand, following procedures and matrix algorithms for a level of standardization, could easily take eight to twelve hours. Nevertheless, with consistent interest and application, attention to the development of network analysis reemerged in the 1970s, with the advancement of computer-based analysis techniques (Bonanich, 1972; Breiger, 1988, 1991; Burt, 1982; Freeman, 1979, 1988; Freeman, Roeder, and Mulholland, 1980). Interest and development have continued since that time.

Current SNA methodological procedures and techniques, then, result from the convergence of several influences. Historically, these include the work of individuals who laid the groundwork and developed foundational strategies, such as Beum and Brundage in sociometrics (1950); Festinger (1949), Forsyth and Katz (1946), Katz (1947, 1953), and Luce and Perry (1949) in the analysis of sociometric data using matrix techniques; Bavelas (1948) in understanding the mathematical models of group structures; and Hage and Harary (1983), Harary (1969), Harary, Norman, and Cartwright (1965), Lorrain and White (1971), and Everett, Boyd, and Borgatti (1990) in the fields of mathematics, graph theory, and graph theoretic applications. The early traditions identified basic structural concepts such as isolates, cliques, density, and centrality (Bales, 1950; Lindzey and Borgatta, 1954), while equivalences (the analysis of actors who portray similar roles within subsets) and blockmodels (a method for grouping actors into discrete subsets to identify relationships among subsets) are the result of relatively more recent research and investigations (Arabie, Boorman, and Levitt, 1978; Burt, 1982; Doreian, Batagelj, and Gerligoj, 1994; Lorrain and White, 1971).

General Concepts of Network Analysis

Network analysis is unique in the social sciences in that it focuses on the patterns of the relationships between actors, not on the individual characteristics of those actors. Actors can be individuals, groups, organizations, or some other formation of individuals who interact with one another. Network analysis also looks at multiple levels of analysis. This type of investigation provides the ability to examine both macro- and microlinkages between actors in a quantitative, qualitative, and graphical approach. The interaction between actors is the ultimate unit of analysis (Kilduff and Tsai, 2003).

Network researchers have generally focused on specific issues within the field. Krackhardt and Brass (1994) have concentrated on the intraorganizational aspects of networks, while Baker and Faulkner (1993) have taken the more global approach of studying interorganizational relations as part of the total network field. Uzzi (1997) has studied private sector business ties and their impact on firm profitability, relating network development with performance. Granovetter (1985) has looked at individuals' job networks and their importance in job placement, as well as the embeddedness of network transactions within social and economic interaction. Burt (1982) has focused on structural holes—the openings between actors that share no relationship—and the opportunities they create within the business field.

Other applications of network analysis within the social sciences have been more diverse, as illustrated by research on an array of topics: community elites (Laumann and Pappi, 1976), interorganizational relationships in health and human services organizations (Bolland and Wilson, 1994), social support networks (Barrera, Sandler, and Ramsay, 1981; Vaux, 1988), the diffusion of family planning methods in Korean villages (Rogers and Kincaid, 1981), the spread of disease in HIV/AIDS research (Bond and Valente, 1996; Klovdahl and others, 1996; Wright and Myers, 1996), communication research (Rogers and Kincaid, 1981), political networks (Mizruchi and Potts, 1996; Mardon, 1996), social influence (Burt and Uchiyama, 1989; Friedkin and Johnsen, 1990), and even the U.S. Supreme Court (Han and Breiger, 1996).

There are three primary lines of investigation using SNA: (1) the total structure, (2) the subsets formed within the total group structure, and (3) the "points," "vertices," "nodes," or individuals who comprise the network (Burt, 1982; Knoke and Kuklinski, 1982; Rogers and Kincaid, 1981). In other words, the parts making up the whole, either individually or in clusters, or the entire network itself can be the unit of analysis. The important concepts when considering the complete network include these:

- *Dyad:* Two actors who have a connection, a relationship
- *Clique:* A subset of actors within a network who have ties with all other actors within that subset
- *Density:* The proportion of the total available ties connecting actors
- *Centralization:* The fraction of main actors within a network
- *Reachability:* The number of ties connecting actors
- *Connectedness:* The ability of actors to reach one another reciprocally, that is, the ability to choose a relationship between both parties
- *Asymmetry:* The ratio of reciprocal relationships—those relationships that are mutual—to total relationships within a network
- *Balance:* The extent to which ties in the network are direct and reciprocated

These concepts are measured through the use of algorithms (for example, density) or explored and understood through structural elements such as dyads and cliques. For example, reachability is a measure of dyads, and connectedness can be measured by components, cliques' co-membership, and a variety of other tools.

At the individual level of analysis are these key notions:

- *Centrality:* The degree to which an actor is in a central role in the network
- *Homophily:* The degree to which similar actors in similar roles share information
- *Isolate:* An actor with no ties to other actors
- *Gatekeeper:* An actor who connects the network to outside influences

- *Cutpoint:* An actor whose removal results in unconnected paths in the network

All measures, whether on the macro- or microlevel, help to characterize network properties (Kilduff and Tsai, 2003).

There is debate as to whether network analysis is a theoretical field unto itself or merely a collection of methodologies that can be used in the study of social relations. Prominent researchers in the field generally work in one of three categories. Developed from the lineage of early network scholars, the first category includes work based on mathematics (graph network theory) or social psychology (balance and social comparison theory). The second category is a collection of ideas that have emerged from within the field of network analysis itself. These include the concept of heterophily, which looks at the strength and opportunity of ties, and structural holes and structural role theory, which analyzes the overall structure of the actors in a network and their potential influence. The third category encompasses the use of network approaches in other subject areas. Network ideas have been readily used with organizational theories that include contingency theory, population ecology, institutionalism, and resource dependency theory (Kilduff and Tsai, 2003). Network concepts have provided increased robustness and a social orientation within some organizational theories.

This social orientation includes conceptualizations of complexity and systems. Historically, computer-based analysis, built on complex algebraic, matrix, or graph theoretic models, was designed to address the need to mathematically quantify and represent the structural conceptualizations of networks. But beyond this level of analysis on network structure is the specific characteristic of network analysis, which is that "it cannot be solved by the incremental accretion of information, observation by observation, as [many] other statistical problems are. Rather it requires an overview of an entire structure" (Rogers and Kincaid, 1981, p. 71). In other words, SNA is not linear. The specific characteristics of network analysis—what Wellman (1988) refers to as structural analysis—that differentiate it from traditional methodologies and guide inquiry are the following: analysis is focused on relations, not categories of attributes, and on the pattern of relationships among the network, not the accumulation of member relationships; structure may be partitioned into discrete groups; and the focus is on the limits and opportunities of that structure. Although some computer procedures for doing network analysis incorporate algorithms used in more traditional data analysis procedures (for example, factor analysis and multidimensional scaling), the differences are in the purpose for the analysis, the conceptualization of the data, and the incorporation of the results of the analysis.

The development of computer-assisted analysis has led to major advances in understanding the properties of structural components. This understanding of structure, which can be aligned to the evolving develop-ment of organizational and program theories of complexity and systems, has sometimes been in advance of the corresponding theories that describe net-work structure within organizations and programs. Durland (1996) explains that three components have often preceded a theory about what these com-ponents mean or reveal about the network structures being investigated: (1) the clarification, delineation, and explanation of the structural components that describe the patterns found in networks (such as isolates, dyads, wheels, and chains); (2) the structural and mathematical relationships of the components to each other; and (3) the algorithms for identifying these structural components (Holland and Leinhardt, 1979; Rogers, 1987).

With the current direction and focus in evaluation for addressing issues of complexity and structure, the potential for the application of SNA is dra-matic. The complexity of the methodology and the diversity of the applica-tions have provided a beginning theory of social structure (Freeman, 1989), but this theory is far from complete. The theory does begin to provide a framework for decision making in the application of SNA. For example, contextual relationships can be identified. The contextual relationships explored through network analysis have included power structures, social support networks, communication networks, friendship networks, diffu-sion networks, kinship networks, corporate networks, community elites, and exchange networks. Context is critical for the application of SNA: it provides the theoretical framework from which to develop the evaluation questions and the measures that align to that theory.

In addition, there are the empirical structures identified by Cartwright and Harary (1979). These are seven levels of empirical structures that they label: cognitive elements, persons, social roles and positions, groups and organizations, nations, tasks, and variables. The context of a structure (the conceptual and theoretical framework of an evaluation design), crossed with these empirical structures (levels of analysis), forms a matrix (levels of analysis crossed with contextual framework) for sorting the variety of research agendas that have been explored or are possible to explore and pro-vide a framework for developing evaluation questions.

The tools of SNA, the structural components like dyads, and the math-ematical algorithms and lines of investigation—network, subgroups, or indi-vidual—are used to describe and define the parameters of each of the empirical structures within the context of one or more theoretical struc-tures. In other words, the tools of network analysis and the lines of investi-gation can be applied within each cell of the matrix formed by theory and level of analysis. In addition, within a specific study, it is common to explore multiple lines of investigation with multiple tools.

This decision-making process for the application of SNA to evaluation questions makes it more complex than creating a data collection design for a specific statistical analysis such as an analysis of variance. Nevertheless, it is a framework that can be aligned to the more complex questions people may ask about programs, such as whether the program even has the structural capacity to enact its activities and events in ways that support success. SNA is a dynamic process that engages the evaluator and pushes the understanding of complexity and systems to the forefront, providing new clues on how programs work.

References

Arabie, P., Boorman, S. A., and Levitt, P. R. "Constructing Blockmodels: How and Why." *Journal of Mathematical Psychology,* 1978, *17,* 21–63.

Baker, W., and Faulkner, R. "The Social Organization of Conspiracy: Illegal Networks in the Heavy Electrical Equipment Industry." *American Sociological Review,* 1993, *58,* 837–860.

Bales, R. F. *Interaction Process Analysis: A Method for the Study of Small Groups.* Reading, Mass.: Addison-Wesley, 1950.

Barrera, M., Sandler, I. N., and Ramsay, T. B. "Preliminary Development of a Scale of Social Support: Studies on College Students." *American Journal of Community Psychology,* 1981, *11,* 133–143.

Bavelas, A. "A Mathematical Model for Group Structures." *Applied Anthropology,* 1948, *7,* 16–30.

Beum, C. O. Jr., and Brundage, E. G. "A Method for Analyzing the Sociomatrix." *Sociometry,* 1950, *13,* 141–145.

Bolland, J. M., and Wilson, J. V. "Three Faces of Integrative Coordination: A Model of Interorganizational Relations in Community-Based Health and Human Services." *Health Services Research,* 1994, *29*(3), 341–366.

Bonacich, P. "Communication Dilemmas in Social Networks: An Experimental Study." *American Sociological Review,* 1990, *55,* 448–459.

Bond, K. C., and Valente, T. W. "Beds, Bars, and Bridges: Social and Sexual Networking in Urban Northern Thailand." Paper presented at the International Sunbelt Social Network Conference Annual Meeting, Charleston, S.C., Feb. 22–25, 1996.

Breiger, R. L. "The Duality of Persons and Groups." In B. Wellman and S. D. Berkowitz (eds.), *Social Structures: A Network Approach.* Cambridge: Cambridge University Press, 1988.

Breiger, R. L. *Explorations in Structural Analysis: Dual and Multiple Networks of Social Structure.* New York: Garland Press, 1991.

Burt, R. S. *Toward a Structural Theory of Action: Network Models of Social Structure, Perception, and Action.* Orlando, Fla.: Academic Press, 1982.

Burt, R. S., and Uchiyama, T. "The Conditional Significance of Communication for Interpersonal Influence." In M. Kochen (ed.), *The Small World.* Norwood, N.J.: Ablex, 1989.

Cartwright, D., and Harary, F. "Balance and Clusterability: An Overview." In P. W. Holland and S. Leinhardt (eds.), *Perspectives on Social Network Research.* Orlando, Fla.: Academic Press, 1979.

Doreian, P., Batagelj, V., and Gerligoj, A. "Partitioning Networks Based on Generalized Concepts of Equivalence." *Journal of Mathematical Sociology,* 1994, *19*(1), 1–27.

Durland, M. M. "The Application of Network Analysis to the Study of Differentially Effective Schools." Unpublished doctoral dissertation, Louisiana State University, 1996.

Everett, M., Boyd, J. P., and Borgatti, S. P. "Ego-Centered and Local Roles: A Graph Theoretic Approach." *Journal of Mathematical Sociology,* 1990, *15,* 163–172.

Festinger, L. "The Analysis of Sociograms Using Matrix Algebra." *Human Relations*, 1949, *2*, 153–158.

Forsyth, E., and Katz, L. "A Matrix Approach to the Analysis of Sociometric Data: Preliminary Report." *Sociometry*, 1946, *9*, 340–347.

Freeman, L. C. "Centrality in Social Networks: Conceptual Clarification." *Social Networks*, 1979, *1*, 215–239.

Freeman, L. C. "Computer Programs and Social Network Analysis." *Connections*, 1988, *11* (2), 26–31.

Freeman, L. C. "Social Networks and the Structure Experiment." In L. C. Freeman, D. R. White, and A. K. Romney (eds.), *Research Methods in Social Network Analysis*. Fairfax, Va.: George Mason University Press, 1989.

Freeman, L. C., Roeder, D., and Mulholland, R. R. "Centrality in Social Networks: II. Experimental Results." *Social Networks*, 1980, *2*, 119–141.

Friedkin, N. E., and Johnsen, E. C. "Social Influence and Opinions." *Journal of Mathematical Sociology*, 1990, *15*, 193–206.

Granovetter, M. "Economic Action and Social Structure: The Problem of Embeddedness." *American Sociological Review*, 1985, *91*, 481–510.

Hage, P., and Harary, F. *Structural Models in Anthropology*. Cambridge: Cambridge University Press, 1983.

Han, S., and Breiger, R. L. "Switching and Stacking: Network Multiplexity in the Supreme Court." Paper presented at the International Sunbelt Social Network Conference Annual Meeting, Charleston, S.C., Feb. 22–25, 1996.

Harary, F. *Graph Theory*. Reading, Mass.: Addison-Wesley, 1969.

Harary, F., Norman, R. Z., and Cartwright, D. *Structural Models: An Introduction to the Theory of Directed Graphs*. Hoboken, N.J.: Wiley, 1965.

Holland, P. W., and Leinhardt, S. "Structural Sociometry." In P. W. Holland and S. Leinhardt (eds.), *Perspectives on Social Network Research*. Orlando, Fla.: Academic Press, 1979.

Katz, L. "On the Metric Analysis of Sociometric Choice Data." *Sociometry*, 1947, *10*, 233–241.

Katz, L. "A New Status Index Derived from Sociometric Analysis." *Psychometrika*, 1953, *23*, 39–43.

Kilduff, M., and Tsai, W. *Social Networks and Organizations*. Thousand Oaks, Calif.: Sage, 2003.

Klovdahl, A. S., and others. "Large Social Networks of Minority Adolescents: Random Walks Through Populations in Atlanta and San Juan." Paper presented at the International Sunbelt Social Network Conference Annual Meeting, Charleston, S.C., Feb. 22–25, 1996.

Knoke, D., and Kuklinski, J. H. *Network Analysis*. Thousand Oaks, Calif.: Sage, 1982.

Krackhardt, D., and Brass, D. "Interorganizational Networks: The Micro Side." In S. Wasserman and J. Galaskiewicz (eds.), *Advances in Social Network Analysis*. Thousand Oaks, Calif.: Sage, 1994.

Laumann, E. O., and Pappi, F. *Networks of Collective Action: A Perspective on Community Influence Systems*. Orlando, Fla.: Academic Press, 1976.

Lindzey, G., and Borgatta, E. F. "Sociometric Measurement." In G. Lindzey (ed.), *Handbook of Social Psychology*. Reading, Mass.: Addison-Wesley, 1954.

Lorrain, F., and White, H. C. "Structural Equivalence of Individuals in Social Networks." *Journal of Mathematical Sociology*, 1971, *1*, 49–80.

Luce, R. D., and Perry, A. D. "A Method of Matrix Analysis of Group Structure." *Psychometrika*, 1949, *14*(1), 95–116.

Mardon, A. A. "Importance of Networks Among Alberta Politicians." Paper presented at the International Sunbelt Social Network Conference Annual Meeting, Charleston, S.C., Feb. 22–25, 1996.

Mizruchi, M. S., and Potts, B. P. "Centrality and Power Revisited: Actor Success in Group Decision Making." Paper presented at the International Sunbelt Social Network Conference Annual Meeting, Charleston, S.C., Feb. 22–25, 1996.

Moreno, J. L. *Who Shall Survive? Foundations of Sociometry, Group Psychotherapy, and Sociodrama.* Washington, D.C.: Nervous and Mental Disease Publishing Co., 1934.

Radcliffe-Browne, A. R. *Structure and Function in Primitive Society: Essays and Addresses.* New York: Free Press, 1959.

Rogers, E. M. "A Note on Strangers, Friends, and Happiness." *Social Networks,* 1987, 9, 311–331.

Rogers, E. M., and Kincaid, D. L. *Communication Networks: Toward a New Paradigm for Research.* New York: Macmillan, 1981.

Scott, J. *Social Network Analysis: A Handbook.* (2nd ed.) Thousand Oaks, Calif.: Sage, 2000.

Uzzi, B. "Social Structure and Competition in Interfirm Networks: The Paradox of Embeddedness." *Administrative Science Quarterly,* 1997, 42, 39–67.

Vaux, A. *Social Support: Theory, Research, and Intervention.* New York: Praeger, 1988.

Warner, W. L., and Lunt, P. S. *The Social Life of a Modern Community.* Yankee City Series, Vol. 1. New Haven, Conn.: Yale University Press, 1941.

Wellman, B. "Structural Analysis: From Method and Metaphor to Theory and Substance." In B. Wellman and S. D. Berkowitz (eds.), *Social Structure: A Network Approach.* Cambridge: Cambridge University Press, 1988.

Wright, E. R., and Myers, J. "Peer-Based HIV Risk Reduction: A Network Approach to Assessing the Nature and Dynamics of Peer Influence." Paper presented at the International Sunbelt Social Network Conference Annual Meeting, Charleston, S.C., Feb. 22–25, 1996.

KIMBERLY A. FREDERICKS *is assistant professor of public administration and policy in the Department of Political Science, Indiana State University.*

MARYANN M. DURLAND *is an independent consultant specializing in evaluation and the applications of social network analysis.*

3

This chapter provides an overview of the methodology of social network analysis (SNA) and a framework for understanding the next four chapters, which are case studies illustrating the application of SNA.

Exploring and Understanding Relationships

Maryann M. Durland

Although the process of doing social network analysis (SNA) is similar to traditional research and evaluation design, it is in the details that the two traditions diverge. This chapter describes two areas of differences: (1) the framework for doing SNA and (2) data collection, analysis, and specific measures. SNA looks and sounds different from traditional methodologies (Hanneman, 2001). Two examples are the array of data and the language of analysis. At the data level, conventional data consist of columns of measurements on an attribute variable and rows of cases or subjects. This data analysis array is rectangular. The language of conventional analysis consists of terms such as *scores*, comparison of how subjects are similar or dissimilar across variables or how the variables are similar or dissimilar across the subjects. Network data have a square array. The rows, as in conventional data, are subjects or actors. The columns are the same set of actors. The measurement in each cell is the measure of the existence or degree of a relationship between the two actors. Though network analysts make row and column comparisons similar to conventional analysis, what is different is the holistic analysis of the data. The language of SNA includes terms such as *density, cliques,* and *block models.*

SNA is about relationships and how to measure them. Results are in the form of both numerical data and a visual image called a *sociogram* or *social map.* Figure 3.1 is an example of a graph that illustrates the relationship among four individuals. Graphs are the building blocks for sociograms and

NEW DIRECTIONS FOR EVALUATION, no. 107, Fall 2005 © Wiley Periodicals, Inc.
Published online in Wiley InterScience (www.interscience.wiley.com) • DOI: 10.1002/ev.159

Figure 3.1. Graph of a Simple Relationship

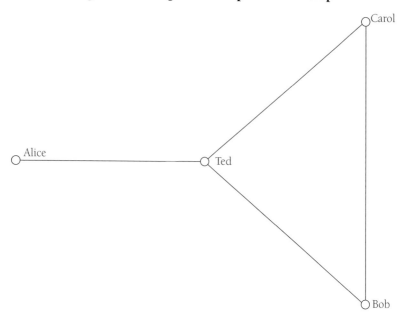

for understanding SNA data. This graph shows that the relationship, which could be friendship (With whom do you prefer to go to the movies?) or trust (Which team member would you prefer to represent you on the grievance committee?), is nondirectional.

In a nondirectional graph, we cannot tell who indicated the relationship; we know only that a relationship exists to some degree. In this graph, there is a connection between Ted, in the middle, and everyone else, and Alice is connected only to Ted. Figure 3.2 shows the same network, but this time it is a directed graph. With arrows, we can see that Alice and Ted both indicate that there is a relationship and that Bob indicates a relationship with Carol, which she does not reciprocate. Figure 3.3 exemplifies a third dimension of graphs: a value to the relationship. In this figure, the darker the lines are, the higher the value is of the relationship. Value can be determined in many ways, such as by ranking (Whom would you choose first?). Each direction of the relationship, with the addition of a value, contributes to the shade of the line.

These graphs provide some level of information about these individuals and the measured relationship, but graphs are just the beginning of the process. Graphs and sociograms illustrate the relationship but do not provide an understanding of the relationship or answer any relationship questions, such as who is the most popular of your friends or who is the most trusted person to put on the grievance committee. In small graphs such as

Figure 3.2. Graph with Direction of a Relationship

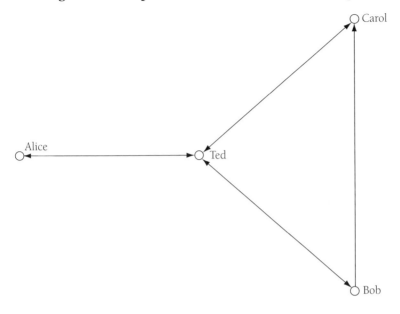

Figure 3.3. Graph with a Valued Relationship

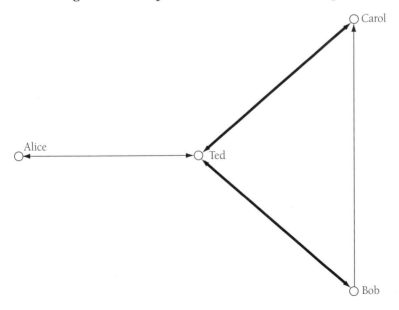

this one, we can perhaps see what is going on and answer those questions, but most times there are many more individuals in the network, and the analysis is more complicated than a visual inspection will explain.

This chapter explores some of the processes for doing SNA, as illustrated in the case chapters that follow. It describes how graphs such as these are the foundation for understanding social network data, what those data look like, and the other tools of SNA methodologists. Examples from the cases are provided throughout this chapter.

SNA Framework

Three important characteristics underscore and provide a framework for doing SNA: a relationship can be defined, a network can be identified that the relationship can be placed on, and the relationship can be measured.

Relationships. SNA is used to explore networks through the lens of a specific relationship or relationships. This relational identity and the relational information in the form of data create the network structure (that is, the lines connecting the shapes that represent the people, organizations, departments, and so on). Relationships range from family marriages to money lenders, gangs to club memberships, friendship to support.

The relationships for the cases presented in this volume concern communication and knowledge relationships and include communication about work over a specific period of time in a specified manner in the cases in Chapters Four and Seven, organizational connections in Chapter Five, and knowledge experts in Chapter Six. In a relational evaluation, the measure is the existence of or the degree of a specific relationship between two members of the network, and generally the direction of the relationship can be in either or both directions, from each member to the other. In most cases, the data collected on the relationship are binary—1 if there is a relationship, and 0 if there is not. For some kinds of analyses, valued data can be used, such as the frequency of communication by day, week, month, or quarter, and the direction (positive or negative) and intensity (for example, friend, acquaintance, knowledge of, stranger) of the relationship.

Developing relational questions follows a natural process for evaluators. Within the context of each evaluation, we determine evaluation questions from many sources, including program logic models, evaluation models, program goals and objectives, stakeholder needs and interests, and from the components of the program itself. Moving from attribute-focused to relational-focused questions is a next step. Typical relationships that apply to evaluation applications include those represented by the four case studies in this volume: who talks to whom, who works with whom, and who do you know who is an expert on a specific topic. However, for each of the cases, there was a specific definition for the relationship, defined by the context of the evaluation, and there was a measure chosen that aligned to that definition; this alignment is explained later in this chapter.

Relationships can be defined simply, as in Chapter Four, or more complexly, as in Chapter Seven. In Chapter Four, Kochan and Teddlie defined the communication relationship as teachers talking to each other during the course of a typical school day. They collected the data by asking teachers whom they talked to during a typical day. In the case in Chapter Seven, Durland first defined the communication relationship as those whom individuals had communicated with over a defined period of time. In addition, members of the network were asked to select the top three people they communicated with about work. Combining the two questions resulted in valued data on communication about work.

In the case in Chapter Six, the relationship was defined as a knowledge information question. Birk asked members of the targeted network to identify individuals with expertise on forty-seven areas of knowledge. This type of question is based on an assumption that individuals work closely with others both within and external to a specific organization and are aware of expertise that may not be commonly known or that has not been organizationally identified or used before. In this case, each question was defined as a relationship: who is the expert on knowledge 1, knowledge 2, and so on. The questions went from more common knowledge to highly specific knowledge. Relationships can be defined on the individual level or the organizational level; the case in Chapter Five is illustrative of relationships at the organizational level.

Networks. A network defines the boundaries within which a relationship will be measured. According to Wassermann and Faust (1994, p. 20), "A social network consists of a finite set of actors and the relation or relations defined on them." The basis of a social network is a set of actors or members, such as people or organizations, who form dyads (one-to-one connections), triads (a subset of three actors), and other combinations of connections that form subgroups, larger clusters or groups, and ultimately the total network. In most applications, the network will be finite, as defined by Wasserman and Faust. But in other cases, the population for the network may not be clearly defined or known, or the network will be a sample of a population. In some cases, the relationship defines the network; in other cases, a network exists on which a relationship will be measured. For example, online dating networks are defined by the relationship, but in evaluations of a school faculty, the network is defined by the members of that faculty. In online dating, the members of the network are identified because they participate in that activity, measured by membership and communication within an online dating group.

In the case in Chapter Four, Kochan and Teddlie worked with a faculty at one school, which forms the network. In the case in Chapter Five, the network was formed from sets of organizations, again a finite number. In the final case, in Chapter Seven, Durland evaluated a network of 213 individuals from two business groups. These three cases illustrate more traditionally defined finite networks. In each of these cases, a specific network—individuals or organizations—had been identified as the target group for the relationship questions.

The case in Chapter Six began with a finite group of thirty-eight members but allowed the addition of other members. This case illustrates how networks develop without preset boundaries. Birk asked members to identify knowledge experts, which resulted in some identified experts residing outside the original network and therefore not responding to the survey. Her focus was not only to understand the current placement of knowledge experts within a given network, but also to evaluate if the existing network even contained the knowledge experts and, if not, whether there were links to find these experts. As a result, there were forty-seven networks, one for each question, and a total network created from the current members of the targeted network and all the other individuals added from each of the forty-seven questions, for a total of forty-eight networks.

Measuring the Relationships. After defining the relationships and identifying the network, the next step is to select measures that align to the specific relationship. In the case in Chapter Four, Kochan and Teddlie defined the network as the school faculty, and the relationship was, "Whom do you talk to in the course of a typical day?" Three measures were selected. For "whom do you talk to," the measure was the indegree centrality. *Indegree centrality,* a measure of popularity, is the number of times others chose the individual. To determine if any individual might be a connector or a barrier within the network, the measure *betweenness centrality* was used, and to identify tight clusters, *clique analysis* was used. *Betweenness* is a measure of the degree an individual is between others, and *cliques* are subgroups where all members connect to each other. Indegree and betweenness are both centrality measures; they indicate how central an individual is to the network. For indegree centrality, *central* means the most popular person, that is, the person who got the most selections. Centrality is an indicator of who can control a network and how he or she might be able to do this. A person who is popular connects to more members in the network than others, and this strong path of links is an indication of power. A person who is popular could be thought of as a star; the popular person is the hub, and each connection is a link. *Betweenness centrality* means that an individual may not be the most popular but is indirectly connected to others. A person with a high betweenness score is under the surface of a network. These people can get to others indirectly through the connections that they have; they are on paths that provide opportunities to others, even if they are not directly connected to those others. They hold power through influence. Individuals who have high indegree may not have high betweenness, and vice versa.

The algorithms used to calculate each of these and many other centrality scores are based on the definition of centrality for that measure. How the evaluator defines centrality is based on how communication or the connection is defined in the evaluation.

Birk also used indegree centrality in her evaluation in Chapter Six, but she used it as a measure of the level of expertise for an individual. Those individuals chosen more frequently were identified as *experts*. This identification does not mean an absolute characteristic of the individual, but rather the person members of the network know or perceive as having expertise or a connection to the appropriate expert. The identification of an expert within the Birk case is an example of knowledge networks and the application of SNA to information management or knowledge management. In Chapter Five, Fredericks used three measures of centrality to illustrate the differences in *communication control,* defined as direct contact, quick access, and the flow of communication. In Chapter Seven, Durland compared the rankings of individuals on indegree and betweenness on three levels of communication and found that 33 individuals were the most central in the network, with 3 of those the most central on multiple centrality measures. This meant that 33 individuals out of the total of 213 were in power positions, related to controlling communication, and 3 individuals held power consistently no matter how she cut the network or defined communication.

Cliques are clusters or subsets of the network in which every member connects with the other. Clique analysis begins with cliques the size of three members and builds from there. Cliques are tight subgroups, and since all members connect to each other, they are mutual networks: each member confirms the connection of the other. The size of the clique indicates how many members are within the clique. In Figure 3.4, which shows clique co-membership, there are seven cliques. The rectangles are the clique number and the ovals are the individuals who are members of that clique. The arrows go from the clique to the members of the clique. In this example of a school faculty, the ovals represent teachers and the one diamond represents the principal. There are also numerous isolates in this organization, at the bottom right. This sociogram is an illustration of taking the results of an analysis—cliques—and using the results to construct the sociogram. In this sociogram, person 64 belongs to cliques 6 and 2, while in clique 7 there are three individuals who are not connected to the rest of the network of cliques.

Traditional Analysis and SNA

Much of SNA has an academic mathematical background, so the language of the data and analysis is often unfamiliar to traditional methodologists (Hanneman, 2001). One of the first notable differences is in the use of algorithms and statistics. From a quantitative perspective, one of the most basic differences between traditional analysis methods and SNA methods is the

Figure 3.4. Clique Co-Membership Graph

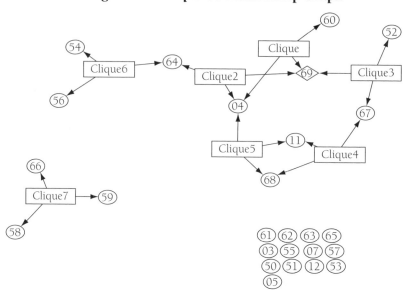

assumptions made about the data or information we want to understand and the assumptions that should be met in order to use a specific statistical analysis. Statistical analyses are techniques and procedures for understanding a set of data or information, whether it is within a traditional or SNA framework. Statistics, at a most basic level, are mathematical calculations ranging from simple to complex to help organize, summarize, and understand data. A statistic, such as computing the mean on a set of data, is the application of an algorithm. Statistics describe both procedures and data. What makes algorithms different from statistics, particularly in the application of SNA, is that generally algorithms are complex, have repeated steps, and may have decision points.

The choice of statistics in traditional methods is based on the characteristics and properties of the data. For example, we calculate means on data that are measured on interval or ratio scales but not nominal. In traditional evaluation and research design, we align sampling, data collection, measures, and data analysis—the choice of which statistics to use—to organize, summarize, explain, or make inferences from the data. Frequency tables summarize, and a *t*-test can determine the level of difference between two groups on the measure used to collect information. In traditional methods, the data collected might be in the form of size, quantity, or quality; on attributes, it might be the level or degree. Traditional data include such things as attendance, grades, scores on a test, participation in a program, hours of training, cars built per day, visits to a clinic, or steps walked.

The premises for doing SNA have a different foundation. For this analysis, the basic data element is the existence of or level of a relationship. This single element is the foundation for creating the networks and the analysis that is chosen. The measures and tools are algorithms, which are similar and in some cases equivalent to statistics. Algorithms are sets of computable steps performed to achieve specific results. For example, a flowchart can represent an algorithm. Algorithms are created based on the conceptual understanding of the relationship, so it is possible that different algorithms will have different steps and instructions yet will end up at the same place. In most cases, SNA methodologists use specific programs such as UCINET (Borgatti, Everett, and Freeman, 1992) and Netminer to work with social network data; experienced researchers may write syntax to calculate the data using traditional statistical analysis programs such as SPSS and SAS.

Another characteristic of doing SNA is that more than one measure generally is used. SNA is more about telling the story of a network with quantitative tools than it is about summarizing, organizing, and determining inferences. SNA is more about understanding the nuances of complexity than about testing a fit or finding a difference or determining common occurrences. For example, in the use of centrality and cliques, part of the analysis of the data and interpretation would be exploring those individuals who were most central and whether they were also members of the cliques; if they were not, further exploration would ask who the members of the cliques were and where the most central individuals were positioned in the network. And what does it mean if the most central individuals are the clique members as opposed to if the most central individuals are not clique members?

Graphs, Matrices, and Sociograms

Social network analysis has traditionally been quantitative in nature, and as Wasserman and Faust (1994) emphasize, there are usually three distinct but related theoretical constructs that form the tools for a network approach to analysis: graph theory, the use of matrices, and sociograms. Each construct provides theory or tools, or both, that contribute to fully understanding a network and network analysis.

Graphs are not the charts that are used to illustrate data in traditional research and evaluation analysis; rather, SNA graphs illustrate the characteristics of the relationship between two or more actors. The matrix or matrices place the network relationships into a format for matrix and algebraic manipulation, and sociograms have traditionally been used to represent or depict the network relationships resulting from both the graphs and the products of matrix manipulations. Graphs have attributes, such as positive and negative values, and there is a set of theoretical premises that forms graph theory. Matrices are the basics for most data collection and data sets,

Figure 3.5. Graph Illustrations Representing Conversations

Note: Circles represent subjects or actors and the lines represent the existence or degree of a connection. Arrows indirect the direction of the connection.

and sociograms either illustrate the network under analysis and the characteristics of the measures, or form another layer of data for qualitative analysis of network characteristics, aligned with the quantitative analysis of the measures. Durland (1996) noted in her work on longitudinally effective and ineffective schools that the sociograms of effective schools appeared to have a more webbed appearance and those of ineffective schools a stringy appearance.

Graphs. The first component of network analysis is the graph that describes a relationship. Every verbal relationship can be defined in a graphic representation. At the most basic level are two actors, A and B, who have a conversation. Figure 3.5 shows the graphs of the possible conversations, not including each actor being silent. The arrows indicate who is talking in the conversation. Either A or B could be talking or sending information to the other, or both could be engaged in the conversation.

As relationships become more complicated with the addition of actors, the graphs represent the dynamics of positions, directions, and positive or negative values. Graphs are not sociograms; they are the building blocks for understanding sociograms. A graph is a set of objects connected by links. The study of graphs in mathematics and computer science is called *graph theory*. It is the principles of graph theory that apply to understanding sociograms. Sociograms are illustrative of a specific social network and are created from data. But what we understand about the sociogram comes from the study of graphs.

A matrix presents the graphic information in a format that can be analyzed with matrix algebra and other processes. The information in the graphs in Figure 3.5 would look like the matrix in Table 3.1. The 0 indicates that there is not a connection or relationship, and the 1 indicates that there is. Social network data are entered across the matrix, so that A has indicated that he or she communicates or has a relationship with B.

Table 3.1. Matrix of Graph Links from Figure 3.5

	A	B	C
A	0	1	0
B	0	0	1
C	1	1	0

Figure 3.6. A Sociogram of the Relationships in Figure 3.5 and Table 3.1

The sociogram puts all the links together to form a network and places them in space in ways that align with the properties of the analysis or with the purpose of the analysis. The sociogram in Figure 3.6 places the relationships indicated in the three graphs and the matrix into a sociogram. The arrows indicate the direction of the relationship. In addition, this sociogram was created with equal lines, or edges, which means that one characteristic of the relationships was kept constant in this particular sociogram.

Sociograms represent a particular network. We can define them as graphic pictures or images of a kind of relationship at a given time. They are constructed with computer programs that use specific algorithms that align to the relationship's parameters to create the graph. The algorithm matches the definition of the relationship and the layout of the data.

Data Collection. As with traditional data collection, SNA data can be collected through observations, interviews, surveys, artifacts, documents, and records. In the case in Chapter Four, data were collected through interviews. In the cases in Chapters Six and Seven, the data were collected through an online survey, with a forced choice or a pick list, which provides a question with everyone in the network listed as selection options. In network surveys, respondents can be provided a pick list, or respondents can be left to name the members in the network or to select a category instead of an actual person. For example, in studies of support networks, it may not be important to know the names of mother, father, sister, or friends, but the classification of the person providing support would be important.

Other networks have been constructed through snowball sampling, where the first individual is asked to name the members of the network under study in interview data, and then the interviewer constructs the network from this information; as each subsequent member is interviewed, the network data and members are added. For example, in a study of diffusion of information, one might ask a doctor to name three other doctors whom he or she would go to for information about new medications. Those three doctors would then be asked the same question. In Chapter Five, Fredericks constructed the network and network data from archival records, as well as from interviews.

Measures and Analysis. Once the data have been collected and entered, they are ready for analysis. Data entry depends on the program that the evaluator is using to analyze the data, but most accept data in the form of a matrix that can be created in a word processing document or a spreadsheet program. This volume does not detail the use of the programs or specifics on data entry, but focuses instead on a broad overview of the measures, analysis, and results. There are three levels of analysis: the total network, subgroups, and the individual. Generally a combination of levels is used in any specific evaluation. In each of the cases in Chapters Four through Seven, we see examples of the total network and subgroups, and in the case in Chapter Five, we see an example of ego networks or individual networks.

Complete Network Measures. Traditional total network measures include density and components. Both measures provide an indication of the overall cohesiveness of the network. Density has long been used as a measure of group cohesion (Wasserman and Faust, 1994). Density is much like an overall degree measure: it indicates how connected the network is in a very broad manner. Density varies from 0 to 1 and is calculated in UCINET IV and 6 as the total number of connections or ties divided by the total number of possible ties. Density can also be calculated for valued data. It should be interpreted with group size, as the larger the group, the more likely that network density will decrease (Wasserman and Faust, 1994). However, density is a popular measure and provides an indication of the level of network connectivity.

Components indicate the overall connectedness of a network. They indicate major breaks or divisions in the network. If there is one component, everyone is reachable. Figure 3.7 illustrates a network with two large components and four isolates. Each isolate is an individual or object that stands alone. In this sociogram, the four isolates are along the left, no names are provided to identify the circles, and the lines indicate the direction of the relationship or who provided the data about the connection.

Centrality. Centrality describes the status, power, or popularity of an individual within a group. A central person is strategically located within a network. Three centrality measures have been used in the cases in this volume: indegree centrality, betweenness centrality, and closeness centrality. Each can be calculated at the network and the individual level, and they provide an indication of how centralized the network is around one individual. Each operational model of centrality assumes a particular structural relationship between the members of the network (Freeman, 1979). Group centralization measures indicate the extent to which one individual is more likely to be central within the network. For the total network, the larger the centralization measure is, the more likely it is that one individual is central and the other individuals are around the edges of the network. Individual centrality provides scores for each individual so that individual comparisons can be made.

Three common measures of individual centrality are (1) Freeman's indegree centrality, (2) Freeman's betweenness centrality, and (3) Freeman's closeness centrality. Freeman's indegree centrality is a measure of network

Figure 3.7. Components Illustrate Breaks in a Network

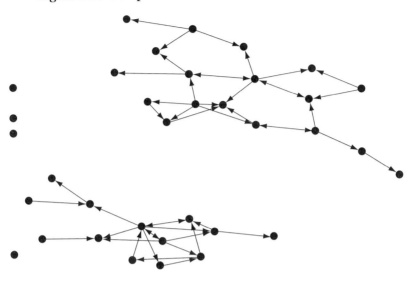

activity and is equal to the number of other members directly linked to a person or the number of times the individual was chosen by others. The normalized degree centrality controls for network size and provides a measure that can be used for comparisons.

Freeman's betweenness is a measure of information control. Betweenness is how much an individual is indirectly linked to other members of the group and is a measure of to what extent an individual is between two others. This measure can also be normalized by taking the betweenness measure divided by the maximum possible betweenness expressed as a percentage.

The third centrality measure is Freeman's closeness, which is a measure of independence from the control of others or how close an individual is to everyone else in the network. This measure has also been described as a measure of efficiency or the ability to get to others without interference, along the shortest possible path available. Persons with closeness are productive in getting communication to others and getting feedback back to them. Closeness is defined as the shortest path (geodesic) connecting one person to another. Individuals can often have many paths to others, and some may be long. A path is the links that it takes to get from one person to another through the network. An individual may be able to get a message to someone, but the message may have to go through many other individuals to get there. This measure looks for those who can get through the network quickly.

Analysis. So far we have mostly touched on sociograms as the results of the analysis of network data, but there are also numerical results. Table

Table 3.2. Centrality Measures

		Degree	Closeness	Betweenness
1	John	3.448	3.956	0.000
2	Bill	6.897	3.978	0.985
3	Gene	10.345	3.989	1.478
4	Jo	6.897	3.978	0.000
5	Ashley	10.345	3.984	0.985
6	Sue	3.448	3.962	0.000

3.2 illustrates the centrality results for a network of six individuals. There are three measures of centrality: degree, closeness, and betweenness. The measures provided are the normalized measures. *Degree* is based on direct links. *Closeness* is based on the shortest paths that connect to others and is a measure of reach. The larger the closeness value is, the longer are the paths to get to others and the less close one is to others. The smaller value indicates a person who is strategically placed to reach others. *Betweenness* centrality measures power in a network. The measure is the proportion of times a person is located on the shortest paths between all pairs of actors. The count is an indicator of how much one person is between all others. To norm the measures, they are expressed as a percentage of the maximum possible connections or paths.

There is little variation in the six individuals on closeness centrality, so no one individual has quicker access or better reach through the network than any other. There are differences, though, on the other two centrality measures. We see that two individuals have degree centrality of 10.345, meaning they have a higher connection to others directly, but only one of these individuals has the highest betweenness score. This means that in a sociogram, these individuals are connected in a different way to others in the network. These numbers are small but provide information on how communication takes place. No one individual has a closeness degree score that would indicate he or she has quicker access through the network, though Gene's is highest on all three measures, which indicates that Gene is a powerful person in this network.

Other Sociogram Characteristics

There are other sociogram characteristics that when combined with data from the measures help to explain the dynamics of a network. For example, bridges and cutpoints illustrate where there are potential breaks in the information paths. Cutpoints are nodes that, if removed, cause the network to break apart or individuals to be disconnected from the network. Bridges are lines that, if removed, cause the network to break apart or individuals to be disconnected

NEW DIRECTIONS FOR EVALUATION • DOI 10.1002/ev

Figure 3.8. Sociogram with Cutpoints and Bridges

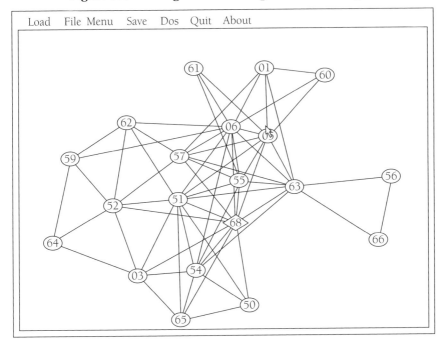

from the network. Bridges and cutpoints can sometimes be seen in cliques that overlap or in components and may indicate weak links, which may indicate barriers, or may be between individuals who facilitate communication or the relationship that is studied. They are two characteristics that indicate how strong or how weak the overall network communication path is. If many individuals can be disconnected from the overall network with the removal of one cutpoint or bridge, then the overall connection is very weak. Bridges and cutpoints can be identified through both data analysis and sociogram inspection. In Figure 3.8, 63 is a cutpoint: removal of this node would disconnect nodes 56 and 66. The line between 63 and 56 is a bridge. In this sociogram of a school faculty, the ovals represent teachers and the diamond represents the principal.

Another dimension of both data analysis and the sociograms is illustrated in Figure 3.9. Sociograms such as this take the analysis and illustrate it. This sociogram, from the case in Chapter Five, is an example of a core periphery structure of a colleague network. Here the core of the network is in the center and has larger nodes; the periphery members of the network are around the core, and the nodes are smaller. The sociogram shows how all of the individuals connect, as well as the intensity of the communication through the data and the sociogram layout.

NEW DIRECTIONS FOR EVALUATION • DOI 10.1002/ev

Figure 3.9. Core Periphery of a Network

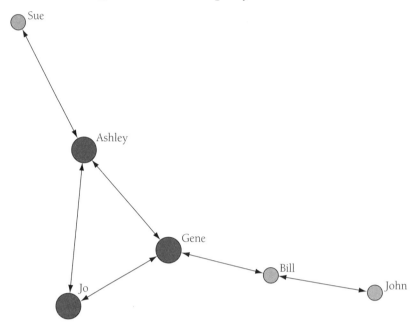

Conclusion

Each of the cases that follows provides examples and more information about doing social network analysis. This chapter has presented an overview of the framework for doing SNA, and the reader is directed to the references after each case study and in the Additional Resources to find more details and information on the measures and the specifics for doing these analyses.

References

Borgatti, S. P., Everett, M. G., and Freeman, L. C. *UCINET IV. Version 1.0 Reference Manual.* Harvard, Mass.: Analytic Technologies, 1992.

Durland, M. "The Application of Network Analysis to the Study of Differentially Effective Schools." Unpublished doctoral dissertation, Louisiana State University, 1996.

Freeman, L. C. "Centrality in Social Networks: Conceptual Clarification." *Social Networks,* 1979, *1,* 215–239.

Hanneman, R. A. *Introduction to Social Network Methods.* Riverside, Calif.: Department of Sociology, University of California, Riverside, 2001. Accessed Oct. 7, 2004, at http://faculty.ucr.edu/~hanneman/SOC157/NETTEXT.PDF.

Wasserman, S., and Faust, K. *Social Network Analysis: Methods and Applications.* Cambridge: Cambridge University Press, 1994.

MARYANN M. DURLAND is an independent consultant specializing in evaluation and in the applications of social network analysis.

4

This chapter focuses on the use of social network analysis in the evaluation of K–12 educational programs.

An Evaluation of Communication Among High School Faculty Using Network Analysis

Susan Kochan, Charles Teddlie

We undertook an analysis of a troubled high school some fifteen years ago (Teddlie and Kochan, 1991). Our original evaluation plan focused on the collection of academic achievement scores and attitudinal variables taken from the school effectiveness literature, but the serendipitous inclusion of what we called sociometric measures resulted in the most valuable information gleaned from the study. Recent reanalysis of the data from the original evaluation study using more sophisticated contemporary social network analysis (SNA) techniques reveals a more complex communication pattern among faculty members than first reported.

Evaluation Context

In education, it is not unusual for a school board to contract with independent researchers to evaluate a school to determine if its students are meeting local and state expectations on key learning outcomes. Often the evaluators conduct an outcomes-based (summative) evaluation that provides objective, confirmatory evidence of what the policymakers already suspected: the school is not performing to standards. Armed with independent, scientific evidence of the school's shortcomings, the board can take action to "fix" the school, protected from criticism that their actions are unjustified or politically motivated.

NEW DIRECTIONS FOR EVALUATION, no. 107, Fall 2005 © Wiley Periodicals, Inc.
Published online in Wiley InterScience (www.interscience.wiley.com) • DOI: 10.1002/ev.160

In this chapter, we describe an evaluation of a troubled high school that was conducted approximately fifteen years ago. In addition to the traditional summative evaluation of student outcomes such as achievement and discipline, we conducted surveys, interviews, and sociometric research as part of a formative evaluation aimed at diagnosing the school's organizational health, and thereby its capacity to adopt and sustain more effective practices.

In October 1989, the president of a rural southern school board commissioned an evaluation into the effectiveness of a local high school embroiled in controversy. In the days before today's pervasive accountability systems, Old River High School (a pseudonym) had been allowed to limp along for years with a record of mediocre student achievement and chronic student misbehavior.

Local dissatisfaction with conditions at the school escalated during the 1988–89 school year and continued into the fall of 1989. Tensions had begun to rise in October 1988 when the principal voluntarily withdrew Old River's football team from the first round of state playoffs after fourteen team members fell short of the state's academic eligibility requirements (a 1.5 grade point average on a 4.0 scale). Angry students responded by organizing a school boycott to protest the principal's actions. Highly visible problems continued at the end of the school year when seven students were arrested in connection with an assault on a teacher's young child in a school hallway. Shortly after, a physical education teacher reported being accosted by a fifteen-year-old student.

As a result of these issues, at the end of the 1988–89 school year, four teachers resigned, and several students withdrew. More important, the combined problems spurred the formerly complacent school board into action. In fall 1989, the board voted to bring in an outside evaluator to determine if there were problems at the school and recommend appropriate improvement strategies to resolve whatever problems were identified.

The Evaluation of Old River High School

For our evaluation, we adopted a mixed-methods model that used both quantitative and qualitative methods to construct attitudinal, behavioral, and cognitive measures of school performance. Our analyses of these data were informed by the extant literature on school effectiveness (Brookover and Lezotte, 1979; Edmonds, 1979; Levine and Lezotte, 1990; Teddlie and Stringfield, 1985; Teddlie, Kirby, and Stringfield, 1989; Teddlie and Reynolds, 2000).

Over the course of four weeks, our team conducted structured interviews with the school's top administrators as well as randomly drawn samples of students, parents, and teachers. We also sampled students and teachers who had left Old River in the wake of the incident, as well as these students' parents. Current administrators, teachers, and students were generally interviewed at the school site; however, we found it necessary to interview some participants at their homes. All field notes and interview transcripts were analyzed in accordance with Lincoln and Guba's guidelines (1985) for qualitative data analysis. In addition, the interview protocol was structured so that some responses could be quantified and analyzed statistically.

Our analysis of administrative data focused on five years of student achievement data from the state testing program, as well as archival data on student attendance, suspensions, and expulsions during the same period. We also conducted schoolwide observations and distributed sociometric questionnaires to all current teachers and administrators.

General Findings from the 1989 Evaluation

Based on our school observations and interview data, we concluded that Old River was an ineffective school characterized by poor instruction, weak leadership, and low student and teacher morale. Our analyses of administrative data further reinforced our perception of Old River as a place where students performed as expected (poorly) and were minimally engaged in school, as evidenced by the high rates of student misbehavior and absenteeism. To round out our evaluation, we analyzed data gathered through the sociometric questionnaires to determine if communication patterns among the faculty supported or contradicted the case that was emerging of an ineffective organization.

Sociometric Findings from the 1989 Analyses

The sociometric research that we conducted in 1989 was modeled after the approach described by Kerlinger (1986, 2000) in his classic research methods texts, which were based largely on the psychological research in social choice and interpersonal attractiveness (for example, Lindzey and Byrne, 1968). To be specific, we used Kerlinger's technique (Kerlinger, 1986) for hand-calculating sociomatrices and sociograms derived from survey responses.

Though primitive by today's technologically sophisticated standards, our sociometric analyses might be considered groundbreaking for the time, at least in the field of education. The 1980s and 1990s witnessed a series of sophisticated advances in sociomatrix analysis that, coupled with remarkable innovations in computer graphics, created a renewed interest in the graphic representation of data. Nonetheless, education evaluators in general (and school effectiveness researchers in particular) were little aware at the time of these advances. True, there had been extensive studies using sociograms to measure student peer relationships in schools (for example, Asher and Dodge, 1986; Smith, 1969; Tyne and Geary, 1980), but little if any research related to social networks among faculty members.

The sociometric questionnaires that we distributed faculty-wide identified every teacher and administrator by name and also posed five work or

Exhibit 4.1. Sociometric Questionnaire Administered to Teachers and Administrators at Old River High School

1. Please list the three persons you would most prefer to work with during the spring semester or on a task force that has been created to study ways of improving the educational environment at this school.
2. Please list the three individuals with whom you would most like to serve during the spring semester on a committee that has been created to tackle student disciplinary problems at this school.
3. In answering the following question, assume that your school has office spaces for all teachers. Please select the three individuals with whom you would feel most comfortable sharing an office space during the coming academic year.
4. Please select the three persons whom you would like to choose to represent you during the coming year on a committee created to improve faculty welfare.
5. Please list the three persons with whom you most prefer to associate in an informal social setting (occasion) after school hours.

social scenarios (see Exhibit 4.1). For each scenario, respondents were asked to identify the three colleagues with whom they would prefer to collaborate or interact.

Fourteen of twenty faculty members returned completed questionnaires, for an overall response rate of 70 percent. From the responses, we generated two scores for each individual: (1) a social receptiveness score, indicating how many times the faculty member had been selected by his or her peers, and (2) a social acceptance score, which reflects the number of times an individual was chosen, as well as his or her order of selection (first, second, or third choice). For example, a teacher chosen by two peers in each of the five scenarios would have a social receptiveness score of 10: $5 \times 2 = 10$.

The weightings for the sociometric status scores were a score of 3 if chosen first, a score of 2 if chosen second, and a score of 1 if chosen third. If the teacher described in the previous paragraph were one colleague's first choice for every scenario and another colleague's second choice in all five instances, the teacher's sociometric status score would be 25: $(5 \times 3) + (5 \times 2) = 15 + 10 = 25$.

The ranges for both the social receptiveness and the sociometric status scores were high, suggesting wide variation in the amount of communication and collaboration among the various members of the organization. Social receptiveness scores ranged from 3 to 23, with an average of 10.3 and a standard deviation of 6.2. We interpreted this to mean that the typical faculty member was chosen by two colleagues in each of the five professional or social scenarios. Sociometric status scores ranged from 4 to 53, with an average of 20.6 and a standard deviation of 14.1.

The diagram in Figure 4.1 was plotted by hand and is based on the social receptiveness scores we calculated. It does not include instances in which a faculty member selected another only once. To have included all

Figure 4.1. Sociogram Based on Social Receptiveness Scores, 1989

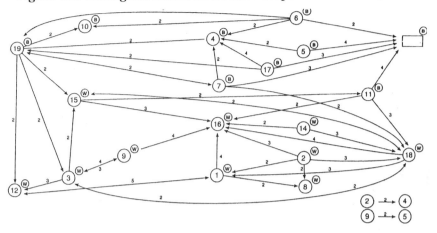

single selections would have greatly complicated the sociogram, yet would have brought little meaningful information to the analysis. We chose to focus on communication links on the receptiveness scores that were equal to or greater than two as indicators of consistent communication. Two interactions were placed in the lower-right-hand corner in a further effort to increase readability.

Arrows point from the individuals who made selections (choosers) to the colleagues they chose. The numeral that appears over the arrow indicates the number of times the colleague was chosen by that particular chooser. Double arrows identify reciprocal relationships (that is, instances in which two colleagues chose each other) and are more significant than one-way relationships. According to Wasserman and Faust (1994), reciprocal relationships are much more reliable indicators of actual social relationships than instances in which only one person chooses the other. For example, one colleague may choose another because he or she identifies with that person or would like to initiate a line of communications without there being an actual relationship between the two.

The principal (number 13 in the diagram) had a social receptiveness score of 20 and a sociometric status score of 41. Both scores were the third highest among the faculty; thus, only two faculty members were chosen more often than the principal and had an equal or higher standing among their peers. Five of the six faculty members who did not return a completed sociometric questionnaire (including the principal) were chosen by other teachers and appear in the diagram. The one teacher who did not return the questionnaire and was not selected by a colleague is not included in the diagram.

As previously noted, reciprocal relationships are judged by some to be the most reliable indicators of well-established relationships. Only five such linkages are apparent in Figure 4.1, and no single person is involved in more than one reciprocal relationship.

In our 1989 interpretation of Figure 4.1, we identified four cliques, each revolving around one of the four individuals with the highest social receptiveness scores: numbers 16, 18, 13, and 4. On closer examination, we determined that two cliques revolved around white staff members and were predominantly white cliques. The other two cliques revolved around black staff members and were predominantly black cliques. We extended our analysis of communications within and between racial groups across the entire organization and determined that 82 percent of all social interactions were within racial groups. Of those, 34 percent were interactions among black faculty and 48 percent were interactions among white faculty. Only 18 percent of faculty interactions cut across racial lines (that is, represented an interaction between a black and a white faculty member).

The interaction patterns of the principal were particularly enlightening. Principals often facilitate the faculty's development of a common vision, encourage collaboration, and inspire high expectations for instruction and achievement (for example, Brookover and Lezotte, 1979; Edmonds, 1979; Levine and Lezotte, 1990). To do so effectively, they must function at the center of the organization.

In contrast, the principal at Old River functioned on the relative periphery of the organization. As noted in Figure 4.1, only five of twenty faculty members (25 percent, all of whom were black) chose the principal. In addition, three of the five faculty members who chose him (numbers 17, 6, and 5) also operated within black-only cliques. As previously noted, Figure 4.1 does not reflect single selection interactions and is therefore a partial representation of communications within the school. Nonetheless, when single selections are included, 90 percent of the principal's interactions still fell within the black faculty.

Reanalysis of the Old River Data in 2004

The technology used in today's SNA is much more sophisticated and insightful than the rudimentary techniques available to education evaluators in 1989. To test our analyses and results based on Kerlinger's algorithms and our hand-drawn diagram against those now computed with computer algorithms, we submitted the sociometric data collected in 1989 to an analyst who specializes in network analysis. Her reanalysis of the 1989 data using UCINET6 (Borgatti, Everett, and Freeman, 2002) and NetDraw (Borgatti, 2002) produced the sociogram illustrated in Figure 4.2 (M. Durland, private correspondence to the authors, 2004).

At a glance, the computer-generated sociogram is much different from the hand-drawn version; however, the two diagrams capture the same core features of the faculty's social network. Faculty members 4, 13, 16, and 18

Figure 4.2. Sociogram Based on 2004 Reanalysis of the 1989 Data

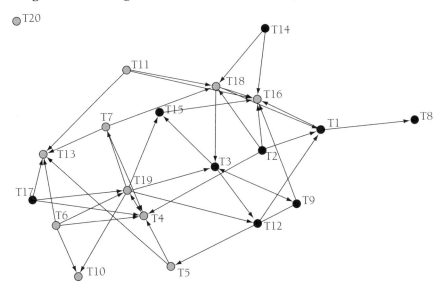

were identified in 1989 as the most critical members of the school's social network, and the reanalysis produced the same finding. In both networks, the principal (number 13) appears on the fringe of the social network, and both diagrams illustrate his preference for communicating through links with black faculty. (White faculty are the dark gray circles, black faculty the light gray circles.) Nevertheless, there are important differences between the diagrams.

The computer-based analysis brings another dimension to the analysis—both literally and figuratively. The network analysis software for generating Figure 4.2 was created with a graph drawing program that allows the analyst to specify network parameters (such as equal or nonequal lines) to create a three-dimensional diagram in which each individual's place within the organization is determined not only by his or her peer choices, but also positions individuals according to the tightness or looseness of their linkages with other members of the organization. For example, in the 1989 sociogram, the principal and faculty member 19 appear on opposite ends of the diagram. The casual reader would interpret this as meaning that the two were distant in their communication patterns. The 2004 sociogram places the two in much tighter proximity, more accurately reflecting faculty member 19's position within a tightly clustered subgroup of black faculty.

We used key concepts from the current social network literature in our 2004 reinterpretation of the Old River data; that is, we looked for four network features: components, isolates, cutpoints, and bridges. Components indicate the overall connectedness of a communication network. The level of connectedness is an indication of the ease with which information typically

New Directions for Evaluation • DOI 10.1002/ev

Figure 4.3. Components, Isolates, Cutpoints, and Bridges in Old River's Social Network

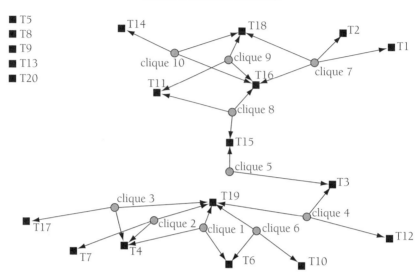

travels across the entire organization. Individuals who are disconnected from the social network are labeled isolates. Both networks reflect that there were isolates at the school, though in the overall network used in the analysis for both years, there is one component. A component is a subgroup of the network that has the maximum number of connected ties (Scott, 2000).

We also looked for cutpoints and bridges. Cutpoints are the members of the organization through whom otherwise disconnected components (subgroups) communicate, and bridges are the path of their communication (represented as the line connecting the "cutpoint" to the "components" that he or she links). Figure 4.3 offers a better illustration of the components, isolates, cutpoints, and bridges in Old River's social network.

Figure 4.3 was generated through a clique analysis of the Old River data and reflects the cliques that formed from the communication links within the group. The diagram is based on a clique analysis with a minimum of three, which measures cliques with a minimum of three members. The resulting co-clique membership matrix was then submitted to NetDraw as affiliation data, and the sociogram was generated. In this sociogram, the circles represent the cliques, and the boxes are the individuals. In affiliation data, each clique represents a row, and the columns are membership in the clique, indicated with a 1 or a 0. The data used to generate Figure 4.2 were the social receptiveness scores in Table 4.1 on which the 1989 sociogram (Figure 4.1) was based. For Figure 4.2, these valued scores were dichotomized. The 2004 reanalysis was more stringent than the original

Table 4.1. Sociometric Receptiveness Scores: 1989 Analysis Compared to Freeman's Indegree Scores, 2004 Reanalysis

Staff Member	1989 Receptiveness	1989 Status	2004 Indegree	1989 Single Selections	2004 Normalized B
T01	6	11	10	0	4.39
T02	5	9	0	5	1.17
T03	14	28	7	7	16.67
T04	17	34	16	1	11.4
T05	9	14	2	7	7.75
T06	7	10	0	7	0
T07	5	10	2	3	2.05
T08	8	15	2	5	0
T09	5	7	4	1	9.65
T10	14	29	4	10	0
T11	4	7	2	2	4.53
T12	13	25	5	8	3.51
P13	20	41	16	4	0
T14	3	4	0	3	0
T15	14	35	4	10	5.56
T16	23	53	22	1	0
T17	3	6	0	3	0
T18	21	42	11	10	13.45
T19	10	23	6	4	18.129
T20	4	9	0	4	0

analysis, however, because it was based on each faculty member's top choices, whereas the original analysis was run on all choices, including the single choices. In the 2004 analysis, the values of the choices equal to or greater than two were used to create the data in the network. However, in 2004, the direction of the link was not a factor in the analysis of the cliques for Figure 4.3. The analysis was run on the broadest interpretation of communication, which was a minimum of a link from one individual to another, which did not have to be reciprocated.

Figure 4.2 (a sociogram) plotted each individual's place within the organization, with individual faculty members represented as circles, connected by lines. Figure 4.3 (based on a clique analysis) graphs the cliques within which members function (represented as circles), with arrows extending from the clique to its members (represented as boxes). According to Figure 4.3, the social network at Old River was composed of ten cliques, functioning within two components. Faculty members 19 and 16 were critical links within the organization, each participating in five and four cliques, respectively. Member 15 was the cutpoint in Old River's social network, connecting the organization's two components. The five individuals who did not return sociometric questionnaires and were not selected by others are arrayed along the left-hand margin of the diagram. These two figures illustrate the complexity of the network depending on the view and what layer of the network is explored. In Figure 4.2 we see the overall communication connections, greater than one, while in Figure 4.3 we see the network from the standpoint of the overlap of members in the smallest groups within the network.

Comparisons were made between the 1989 and the 2004 analyses on the 1989 receptiveness and status measures, the 2004 centrality (Freeman's indegree), and the normalized betweenness score. Freeman's indegree is equal to the receptiveness measure, but in 2004, the single links were not included. Betweenness is a measure of the number of times an individual is a link to another person. The normalized betweenness centrality is the betweenness divided by the maximum possible betweenness expressed as a percentage. The 1989 single selections were determined from the difference between the 2004 indegree and the 1989 receptiveness score, accounting for value. These measures all validated the information from the 1989 analysis, with the betweenness measures indicating 3, 4, 18, and 19 as the individuals with the highest betweenness scores, ranging from 11.1 to 18.1 percent. Individual 15 did not show up with a high betweenness score—it was 5.6 percent—and the location of member 15 within the network and the location in the clique analysis support the low betweenness score.

The 2004 reanalysis reinforces the principal findings from 1989 in that the Old River faculty functioned as two distinct subgroups characterized primarily by race, with a few pivotal members of the faculty linking the two subgroups together. The process of plotting the 1989 sociogram by hand was so laborious and time-consuming, however, that the 1989 team could not accomplish what the network analysis software easily produced in 2004: spatial maps detailing all ten cliques as well as each member's links (ego networks) to other members of the faculty (here omitted for considerations of space).

The 2004 reanalysis therefore yielded information unavailable to the 1989 team when they made their school improvement recommendations to the school board. Had they known in 1989 what was obvious in 2004, the team could have expanded its 1989 general recommendation that a school improvement team be established at Old River by identifying the faculty members whose input would be critical to the team's success.

The Value of SNA to Evaluations Conducted in Educational Settings

The U.S. Department of Education's emphasis on accountability in the use of federal school improvement dollars has triggered a surge in the number of evaluations conducted in educational settings. The federal press for experimental designs—or, at the very least, sophisticated quasi-experimental designs—has given new urgency to the pursuit of scientific approaches to interpreting the organizational complexities of schools.

School effectiveness researchers have long postulated that the schools that are most effective in supporting student learning are led by principals who function as change agents, simultaneously uniting and inspiring the entire school community behind a shared vision that is founded on high expectations for all students. Recent evaluations of the impact of federally funded improvement initiatives also suggest that for schools to reach and maintain high standards of student performance, teachers must work collaboratively across grade levels: continuously observing and providing feedback on each other's teaching, discussing student work, creating opportunities to model instructional innovations, and otherwise supporting each other in a common pursuit of high-quality, pupil-centered instruction (Desimone and others, 2002; Garet and others, 2001). Collaboration at this level requires open communications and high levels of trust throughout the faculty.

More speculative work in the school effectiveness and school improvement traditions suggests that ineffective schools are dysfunctional organizations within which communication gaps, divergent goals, and low levels of collaboration and collegiality impede rational, joint decision making (for example, Myers, 1995; Reynolds and Packer, 1992; Stoll and Fink, 1996; Stoll, Myers, and Reynolds, 1996; Teddlie and Stringfield, 1993). These dysfunctional relationships often arise through the unique social-psychological history of the school (Teddlie and Stringfield, 1993) and have a tendency to continue unless drastic changes (intentional or unintentional) occur.

Sociograms generated through network analysis can be used to study the impact of school reform strategies on the levels and patterns of teacher collaboration and to detect the presence of disconnected cliques, such as those that occur in dysfunctional schools, or conversely that are highly linked and found in schools that are characterized as more effective. Durland and Teddlie (1996) and Durland (1996) used network analysis to analyze the differences between effective (described as "well-webbed") schools and ineffective schools (characterized by cliques or "stringy" structures). Though underused in educational settings, applications of network analyses such as theirs can become an important tool for measuring the instructional capacity of schools and their response to external change agents.

Further evaluation research in this area could develop in several ways:

• More work is needed to refine descriptions of effective and ineffective schools in terms of sociometric measures and sociograms. The hope is that this work will lead to the application of prototypical sociometric measures and the use of sociograms for differentially effective schools.
• Longitudinal sociometric studies should prove useful not only in describing how social relations among faculty change over time, but in exploring the extent to which organizational changes are associated with changes in student outcomes.

• Although it is widely accepted that effective instruction encourages collaborative learning, the classroom observation tools used in most studies of instructional innovations offer only high-level measures of student collaboration. Network analysis of student interactions within classrooms could provide important insights into the nature and extent of student interactions and how those interactions evolve as teachers become more adept at using teaching strategies designed to foster student collaboration.

References

Asher, S. R., and Dodge, K. A. "Identifying Children Who Are Rejected by Their Peers." *Developmental Psychology,* 1986, 22(4), 444–449.

Borgatti, S. P. *NetDraw: Graph Visualization Software.* Harvard, Mass.: Analytic Technologies, 2002.

Borgatti, S. P., Everett, M. G., and Freeman, L. C. *UCINET for Windows: Software for Social Network Analysis.* Harvard, Mass.: Analytic Technologies, 2002.

Brookover, W. B., and Lezotte, L. W. *Changes in School Characteristics Coincident with Changes in Student Achievement.* East Lansing: Institute for Research on Teaching, College of Education, Michigan State University, 1979.

Desimone, L., and others. "Effects of Professional Development on Teachers' Instruction: Results from a Three-Year Longitudinal Study." *Educational Evaluation and Policy Analysis,* 2002, 24(2), 81–112.

Durland, M. M. "The Application of Network Analysis to the Study of Differentially Effective Schools." Unpublished doctoral dissertation, Louisiana State University, 1996.

Durland, M., and Teddlie, C. "A Network Analysis of the Structural Dimensions of Principal Leadership in Differentially Effective Schools." Paper presented at the annual meeting of the American Educational Research Association, New York, April 1996.

Edmonds, R. R. "Effective Schools for the Urban Poor." *Educational Leadership,* 1979, 37(10), 15–24.

Garet, M. S., and others. "What Makes Professional Development Effective? Results from a National Sample of Teachers." *American Educational Research Journal,* 2001, 38(4), 915–945.

Kerlinger, F. N. *Foundations of Behavioral Research.* (3rd ed.) Fort Worth, Tex.: Harcourt, 1986.

Kerlinger, F. N. *Foundations of Behavioral Research.* (4th ed.) Fort Worth, Tex.: Harcourt, 2000.

Levine, D. U., and Lezotte, L. W. *Unusually Effective Schools: A Review and Analysis of Research and Practice.* Madison, Wis.: National Center for Effective Schools Research and Development, 1990.

Lincoln, Y. S., and Guba, E. G. *Naturalistic Inquiry.* Thousand Oaks, Calif.: Sage, 1985.

Lindzey, G., and Byrne, D. "Measurement of Social Choice and Interpersonal Attractiveness." In G. Lindzey and E. Aronson (eds.), *The Handbook of Social Psychology.* (2nd ed.) Reading, Mass.: Addison-Wesley, 1968.

Myers, K. "Intensive Care for the Chronically Sick." Paper presented at the European conference on Education Research Association, Bath, U.K., 1995.

Myers, K. *School Improvement in Practice: Schools Make a Difference Project.* Bristol, Pa.: Falmer Press, 1995.

Reynolds, D., and Packer, A. "School Effectiveness and School Improvement in the 1990s." In D. Reynolds and P. Cuttance (eds.), *School Effectiveness.* London: Cassell, 1992.

Scott, J. *Social Network Analysis: A Handbook.* (2nd ed.) Thousand Oaks, Calif.: Sage, 2000.

Smith, M. "The Schools and Prejudice: Findings." In C. Glock and E. Siegelman (eds.), *Prejudice U.S.A.* New York: Praeger, 1969.

Stoll, L., and Fink, D. *Changing Our Schools.* Bristol, Pa.: Open University Press, 1996.

Stoll, L., Myers, K., and Reynolds, D. "Understanding Ineffectiveness." Paper presented at the annual meeting of the American Educational Research Association, New York, April 1996.

Teddlie, C., Kirby, P., and Stringfield, S. "Effective Versus Ineffective Schools: Observable Differences in the Classroom." *American Journal of Education,* 1989, 97, 221–236.

Teddlie, C., and Kochan, S. "Evaluation of a Troubled High School: Methods, Results, and Implications."Paper presented at the annual meeting of the American Educational Research Association, Chicago, April 1991.

Teddlie, C., and Reynolds, D. *The International Handbook of School Effectiveness Research.* Bristol, Pa.: Falmer Press, 2000.

Teddlie, C., and Stringfield, S. "A Differential Analysis of Effectiveness in Middle and Lower Socioeconomic Status Schools." *Journal of Classroom Interaction,* 1985, 20(2), 38–44.

Teddlie, C., and Stringfield, S. *Schools Make a Difference: Lessons Learned from a Ten-Year Study of School Effects.* New York: Teachers College Press, 1993.

Tyne, T. F., and Geary, W. "Patterns of Acceptance-Rejection Among Male-Female Elementary School Students." *Child Study Journal,* 1980, 10, 179–190.

Wasserman, S., and Faust, K. *Social Network Analysis: Methods and Applications.* Cambridge: Cambridge University Press, 1994.

SUSAN KOCHAN *is coordinator of professional development for the Institute for Child Development, University of Louisiana at Lafayette.*

CHARLES TEDDLIE *is Jo Ellen Levy Yates Professor in the College of Education at Louisiana State University.*

NEW DIRECTIONS FOR EVALUATION • DOI 10.1002/ev

5

This chapter provides a network analysis of a disability demonstration program within a large state and compares its results with the results of a more traditional evaluation of the program.

Network Analysis of a Demonstration Program for the Developmentally Disabled

Kimberly A. Fredericks

This chapter presents the findings from a network analysis of a demonstration program for the developmentally disabled to show the application of graphical network analysis in program evaluation. This case analysis involved interviewing the key stakeholders among the evaluation implementation sites across one state. In addition, evaluation materials such as policies, procedures, and reports were collected and reviewed to supplement the interview information. The sample was a purposive, nonprobability sample of four of the six demonstration program sites that existed within the state and participated in the evaluation.

Background of the Demonstration Program

The developmentally disabled demonstration (DDD) program was a five-year pilot project to provide person-centered service environments to people with developmental disabilities while using an individualized budgeting system for each client. The project originated after two years of planning and discussions between the state agency for the developmentally disabled and local developmentally disabled association affiliates (DDAA). The program was designed to optimize services and supports to consumers while more efficiently using existing resources. The project involved six affiliates of DDAA that agreed to restructure their service delivery systems to provide residential

NEW DIRECTIONS FOR EVALUATION, no. 107, Fall 2005   © Wiley Periodicals, Inc.
Published online in Wiley InterScience (www.interscience.wiley.com) • DOI: 10.1002/ev.161

Table 5.1. Demonstration Site Characteristics

	INC	IR	IM	IU
Number of staff	400	300	1,600	1,500
Number of programs	30	30	60	50
Total consumers served	2,500	2,000	10,000	10,000
Number of consumers in project	130	129	318	152

Note: Due to confidentiality issues, initials indicate the DDD sites.

habilitation, day habilitation, and family support services under the state home and community-based services waiver. The six affiliates were spread across the state in a mix of urban, rural, and suburban service locations. Consequently, there were slight variations in service provision due to regional and consumer demographic differences (see Table 5.1 for characteristics of the sites).

Affiliates provided a number of services, including evaluation, early childhood development centers, day care and universal pre-K, school age education, adult day programs (including day habilitation and day treatment), vocational and supported employment programs, after-school and weekend recreation programs, summer day camp, assistive technology resources, health care (including medical, rehabilitative, dental, audiology, and augmentative communication), residential programs (ranging from community residences to supported apartments to independent living), and family support services (including service coordination, family reimbursement, recreation, after school, overnight respite, and housing and accessibility assistance). Consumers varied within each program, but there were general trends in participants among the programs. Three-quarters of the program consumers received residential habilitation services or day habilitation services or both. Most of the DDD participants were white, with the average age being thirty-seven years. More than half of the consumers (52 percent) had more than one disability. In addition, consumers had considerable motor, communication, and self-care needs within the facilities.

All of the affiliates reported that they chose to participate in the project because they were interested in person-centered planning and providing more individualized services. Under the DDD program, each of the affiliates implemented an individualized budgeting system and trained staff to encourage personal independence, choice, community integration, and inclusion for consumers. A comprehensive evaluation of the program was conducted by the state agency for the developmentally disabled, the Center for Policy Research at the State University of New York at Albany, and the local DDAA organizations. The evaluation project was designed to look at both process (what happened during the project's implementation) and outcomes (the results of the project). The data for the evaluation came from a number of sources:

Outcome indicator surveys, designed specifically for the project and completed by affiliate staff, families, and consumers on an annual basis for the
five years of the project
Developmental disability profile data that track physical and mental indicators for each client
A yearly staff survey (a one-page anonymous survey, completed by affiliate
staff)
Medicaid billing and expenditure data
Periodic site visits by evaluation staff

The evaluation project was guided by the assumption that the implementation of the project would lead to increases in:

• The quality of life for consumers
• Individualization of services for consumers
• Administrative efficiency

In addition to outcome surveys of individual consumers, the DDD project conducted yearly staff surveys to capture attitudes and perceptions from
employees about the services they provided. All direct care, supervisory, and
support staff participated in the survey, which had questions covering three
main areas: perceptions of individualized service, agency support, and consumer choice.

In the end, the evaluation results were mixed. Some affiliates saw statistically significant increases in the quality-of-life and individualization
measures for their consumers after implementation of the program. Others
had previously been providing more individualized services and thus did
not see significant increases in any measures. All of the affiliates failed to
see any administrative efficiency with the implementation of the demonstration program despite reportedly being pleased with the general increase
in the quality of life of consumers.

In the staff surveys over the life of the project, employees responded
favorably to the impact the project had on the services provided to consumers. Yet they struggled to provide individualized services with limited
staff and resources. One staff member suggested that management identify
an array of activities that consumers might choose from and develop direc-
tories of community resources within the site's community. By mapping the
network of each of the affiliates, connections within the community and
among other agencies could readily be identified and further investigated.

During the fourth year of the evaluation, it became apparent that
despite two years of evaluation planning and conducting summative
accountability research with all key stakeholders, the six affiliate sites did
not operate their programs in the same way. Summative accountability
research assesses group performance on certain specified indicators (Flood,

1999). This was the case with the DDD evaluation, as it was one that was comprehensive in nature, reporting results in a summative fashion, and not one that was formative, providing results and recommendations. Two of the local affiliates had already established individualized service networks to a greater degree than their counterparts, which afforded consumers the ability to be more involved in the community. Another affiliate operated its family services program as more of a social gathering rather than a respite program for which it was intended. These differences in programs not only caused measurement error, but the comparisons of measures of programs were at times erroneous. These differences also potentially led to the lack of statistically significant changes in measures for consumers and the full realization of project goals. Despite enacting a comprehensive evaluative approach, implementation sites and evaluation staff within this complex program did not share a common view on each element. Perhaps if there had been agreement on the nature of the program's network, differences might have been more evident.

Recall that system network analysis (SNA) is the study of the relationships among actors. A graphical network analysis maps these relationships and provides a rich description of the program, identifying similar structures, processes, and goals. Similar to a logic model, this systematic view of a program enriches the evaluative process. Network analysis takes a logic model a step further by creating a simplified representation of the system of a program that can be quantified and analyzed mathematically. This type of model elicits the prominence of key stakeholders and differences in program implementation sites. In addition, a graphical analysis allows the investigation of external influences acting on a program, such as other programs or agencies, which can be systematically analyzed. This is a feature that logic models often lack.

In this analysis, staff at four of the six affiliates were interviewed; two of the affiliates declined to participate. The four participating affiliate sites' network was traced to include their relationships with outside agencies at the state and federal levels, along with local and national nonprofit organizations that had an impact on each implementing program. The strength and quality of these relationships were measured to allow the elicitation of important players and the calculation of the density and centralization of each affiliate within the network. These measures illuminate the differences in program processes.

Study Overview

For the case study, I interviewed the directors of four of the six demonstration program sites that participated in the evaluation. As Marsden (1990) noted, this is consistent with the approaches used in other network studies, where often "studies select only one agent to report on an organization's ties to all other organizations" (p. 443). These individuals represent a key actor within the local network and are frequently sampled on a purposive or convenience basis. Furthermore, according to Marsden (1990), "Perceived ties might be more appropriate for studying social influences" (p. 437).

This research approach is often used with ego-centered networks (those around key actors) versus complete networks. In an egocentric design, individual key actors are sampled within the network so as to be representative of the local networks that encompass them, as well as the social settings around the network. This approach is consistent with traditional statistical methodologies for generalizing to larger populations.

Open-ended, semistructured interviews were conducted with each of the four site directors at the local affiliates to gather in-depth information regarding the formal and informal functions of each program, the nature and strength of relationships with outside agencies, and the nature of communication and information flows. Most interviews were sixty minutes in length, and all were tape-recorded for accuracy. I transcribed and coded the data for use in the network analysis. Although the sample was nonrandom and incomplete, it was highly diverse, encompassing a range in size and geographical area across the state and programmatic differences in measures of individualization and quality of life within the evaluation.

Summary of Results

The DDD program network encompassed twenty-two main actors from various levels of government, the public, and the nonprofit sector. The main actors of the network consisted of the DDAA affiliate sites, affiliate boards of directors, state-level oversight and regulatory agencies, federal oversight and regulatory agencies, and local and national nonprofit organizations. Only agencies that were directly involved in the evaluation were interviewed for this study. Figure 5.1 shows the DDD network. These graphical representations of the DDD network were not drawn to scale, but rather were adjusted for readability and comprehensibility of the network. These actors' identification labels were signified by the prefix I for affiliate sites, L for local nonprofits, F for federal-level agencies, S for state-level agencies, BOD for affiliate boards of directors, PR for private agencies, C for county-level nonprofits, and FN for national nonprofits (see Table 5.2). The actors were further identified by a letter in the suffix of the label. In addition, different shapes of nodes represent various types of organizations that were involved in the network.

The DDD network was fairly old and stable by nature. It had been in existence for sixty years, with local affiliates and government agencies being original members of a larger group of disability providers across the state. In general, this network was not perceived to be very political. Although political parties in power at the state level often changed executive-level personnel

Figure 5.1. DDD Network

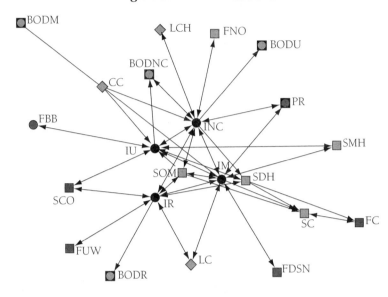

Note: Nodes are identified by organizational type in Table 5.2.

and policies, most of the individuals who provided in-service provision, delivery, and oversight remained relatively constant. An example of this longevity came from the site directors interviewed who stated they had been with their affiliate agency anywhere from ten to thirty years.

The DDD network diagram in Figure 5.1 is a sketch of the main parties involved with the DDD project. This network was constructed through actor interviews, program documents, and anecdotal evidence. The DDD network diagram offers a sense of the size, range, and importance of the

Table 5.2. Actor Descriptions in DDD Network

Network Nodes	Description of Organizational Type
INC, IR, IU, IM	Implementing site: local DDAA agency that implemented the program
LCH, LC	Local site: interacted with some DDAA affiliates to provide services
FNO, FC, FDSN, FUW	Federal site: mostly regulatory and oversight agencies
SMH, SDH, SOM, SC, SCO	State site: mostly regulatory and oversight agencies
BODM, BODU, BODNC, BODR	Board affiliation: agency boards of directors
PR	Private agencies
CC	County-level nonprofits
FN	National nonprofits

Figure 5.2. DDD Valued Network

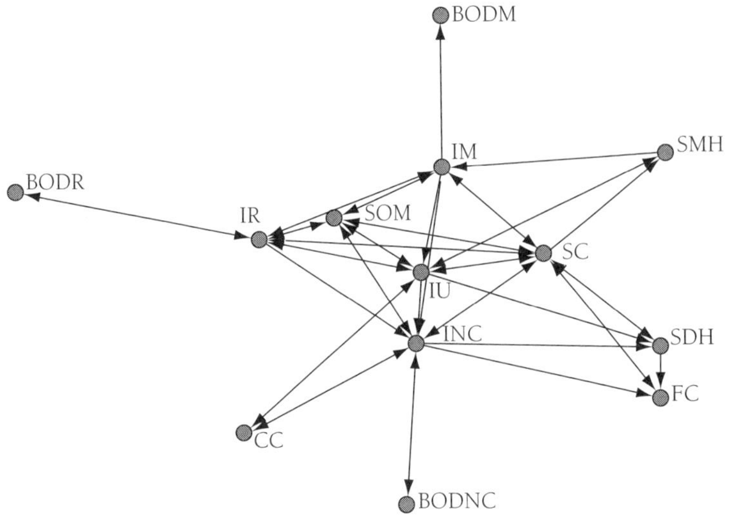

Note: Nodes are identified by organizational type in Table 5.2.

actors involved in the project. Figure 5.1 makes it clear that the program involved a closely knit network with a core group of five actors (INC, IU, IR, IM, and SOM), who were located in the center of the network. These actors occupy a central role in the network as they are involved in several relationships with other actors and are in liaison positions between other pairs of actors. Those actors outside the core hold peripheral positions within the network (Marsden, 2000).

The actors on the periphery were not interviewed for this research because they were not part of the evaluation. This may have caused some interconnections to be omitted from the data; however, there were complete network data for the egocentric networks. As with many other studies, there was limited access to certain people and data outside the purview of the evaluation. In addition, this design is in line with egocentric network data collection. The core-periphery structure is further illustrated through Figures 5.2 and 5.3, which display the valued DDD network and the core and periphery structure of that network, respectively.

The valued diagrams were constructed through interviews with the affiliate directors. The directors were asked not only about the existence of a relationship between known actors, but also about the quality of that relationship. The quality of the relationship was described as positive, negative, or neutral. The valued network had fewer actors, as the site directors commented on only those relationships they felt included enough interactions to evaluate the quality of the relationship.

Figure 5.3. DDD Core-Periphery Structure

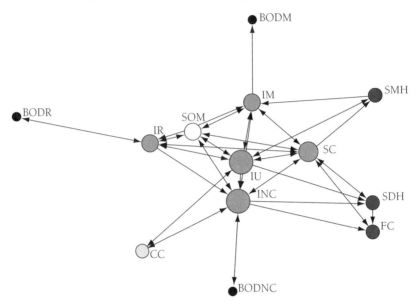

Note: Nodes are identified by organizational type in Table 5.2.

Thirteen actors were identified who had significant valued relationships in this network. These relationships were identified by both reciprocity and quality. Reciprocity encompassed a mutual relationship, shown by arrowheads on both ends of the tie, or a one-way asymmetrical relationship, shown by a single arrowhead pointing in the direction of the flow of the relationship on a tie. Sixty-nine percent of all ties in the network were reciprocal in nature. Thus, the majority of the relationships were symmetrical. Figure 5.3 identifies six core actors (IR, SOM, IM, SC, IU, INC) within the valued network, five of whom were also identified in Figure 5.1: IR, IM, IU, INC, and SOM. Included in this shared group of five were the four affiliate agencies and the state agency for the disabled. The actors with the most influence are represented with the largest size in Figure 5.3. The overlap between the two diagrams makes it clear who the most prominent actors were in this network.

Often core actors are defined by their personal interactions rather than their formal position. These relations reflect the values and attitudes of those actors (Frank, 1995). Perhaps the four implementing agencies were a part of the core structure due merely to the fact that these were the affiliates that were involved in the study. Moreover, it is likely that their agreement to participate in this research demonstrated their similar commitment to individualized planning. Due to their central role in the network, these actors were the hub of information flow to and from other actors in the network.

Yet a closer look at the network reveals that most of the information flow was from the core group to oversight and regulatory agencies or among the core group itself. This would explain the closely knit nature of the network. Further analysis of the data through nonmetric multidimensional scaling (MDS) found a stress level of 0.187, with the core actors of IR, SOM, IM, SC, IU, INC very close together in the center of the network (stress levels under 0.200 indicate a good model fit). MDS analysis allows the representation of proximity among actors to identify which are close to one another (Wasserman and Faust, 1994). This analysis further supported the dense and closely knit nature of this network.

Although there was collaboration in the network, it appeared to be focused among the core actors. This analysis also suggests that both outside influences and resources were kept at the periphery of the network. Not allowing outside information or resources to flow freely into the network would potentially limit the available options for community integration for consumers of the DDD program. As an organization, INC had the highest measure of individualized services and community integration within the evaluation, as well as the largest percentage of reachable ties: 85 percent. Thus, it could directly reach 85 percent of the ties in the network. It was not surprising that it had the highest number of total relationships with other actors and also the most reciprocal ones. Interestingly, INC, IU, and IM, although part of the evaluation and central in the network, were not invited to be on the steering committee for the evaluation. Thus, although they had central roles in the DDD network, they never participated in the planning of the evaluation.

To demonstrate this point further, Table 5.3 reports the normalized centrality measures for the group of actors in the network. The centrality of an actor is the level to which that actor occupies a central role in the network (Wasserman and Faust, 1994). Centrality measures indicate that INC held a strong position in the network. It had a large degree centrality measure of 69, which suggests it was in direct contact with many other actors in the network. These direct connections made INC more accessible to other actors in the network. It also had a high closeness measure, which indicates the ability for this actor to interact quickly with all other actors because of the shorter paths to connection. INC thus had better and faster communication and resource flows both directly and indirectly with the other actors (Monge and Contractor, 2003).

This also permitted INC to create connections within the community and among other agencies for their consumers. INC's high betweenness measure indicates its central role in the network as much of the information flowed through INC to other actors. This could be problematic if INC felt that the information was pertinent only to it or did not want to share

Table 5.3. Centrality Measures for the DDD Valued Network

Actors	Degree	Closeness	Betweenness
INC	69	45	25.6
IU	62	43	10.7
SC	62	43	9.8
IM	54	42	16.2
IR	46	41	14.1
SOM	38	39	0
SDH	31	36	0.4
SMH	23	35	0
FC	23	35	0
CC	15	34	0
BODNC	8	33	0
BODM	8	31	0
BODR	8	30	0
BODU	0		0

resources with other actors in the network because the information would not be dispersed throughout the network. Based on these three measures, it could be said that INC held a broker role in the network, controlling the interaction between two unconnected actors (Marsden, 2000).

The density measures of the network are reported in Table 5.4. Density is a ratio of actual connections between actors as compared to total possible connections (Kilduff and Tsai, 2003). Most actors had a relatively high density measure, which was not surprising for a closely knit and cohesive group of actors involved in the same provision of services and the same project. What was interesting about this network was that the majority of the connections occurred within the core of actors. In previous studies in the mental health field, the networks of providers that were in the lowest-density network were the most effective (Kilduff and Tsai, 2003). The ability to receive information and resources and to maneuver within the network can be constrained in a dense network. This could have been the case with the DDD project.

The ability for the evaluation team to receive information from the affiliates about their programs was limited due to the nature of the network. The sharing of information between other agencies and the affiliates was also hampered. An example of this information asymmetry was discussed when meeting with staff in the third year of the evaluation project. The staff at INC, a small, rural affiliate, spoke of the partnerships they had created with outside agencies to alleviate transportation and community engagement issues they faced with their consumers. The evaluation staff shared this type of success story with other affiliates. One of the affiliates, IM, had no idea of the types of connections INC was making or how it was using staff vehicles to resolve transportation issues.

Table 5.4. Density Measures for the DDD Valued Network

Actors	Size	Ties	Pairs	Density
INC	7	22	42	52.83
SC	7	22	42	52.38
IM	6	21	30	70.00
SOM	5	18	20	90.00
IU	6	14	30	46.67
IR	5	12	20	60.00
SDH	3	5	6	83.33
FC	3	5	6	83.33
CC	2	1	2	50.00
BODU	0	0	0	0
BODNC	1	0	0	
BODM	1	0	0	
BODR	1	0	0	

IM, being in a large city, felt almost embarrassed by its inability to resolve transportation issues when INC could and no longer complained so adamantly about them to the evaluation staff. Yet despite knowing how INC was successful in providing transportation for consumers, IM did not adopt the same procedure. Staff members stated that it was not how they operated and continued with their transportation struggles. But both affiliates were part of the main players in this network and primary actors in information and resource flows. It was surprising that these affiliates did not know about each other's programs and share key practices. This type of information asymmetry allowed the main players in the network—whether or not on purpose—to maintain control and position over the other actors in the network.

Discussion

Overall, the quantitative analysis supported the qualitative findings regarding the link between network structure and program similarities. The closely knit DDD network was dense and relatively small in size. This small, dense structure appears to predict ease of communication of function and processes among the implementation sites within the DDD project. Institutional organization theory would predict that the information diffusion among the network actors would have led to isomorphism, that is, similarity of structure and function among fields of organizations, so that best practices could be used (Brass and others, 2004). In this situation, information and resource flow was partitioned by the central actors clustered together. These actors were tightly connected yet thought of each other as highly dissimilar. Although they shared routine information among the group (for example, meeting times and evaluation activities), they did not share more secondary information of best practices with one another. This finding is contrary to many network studies in which highly dense networks led to ease of information exchange and common frames of reference (see Coleman, 1988; Burt, 1992, 1997; Podolny and Baron, 1997). However, these findings are not unusual within the context of a program evaluation.

Provan and Milward (1995) conducted a study in the mental health field in which they examined four community mental health sites across the United States and collected data on multiple levels (individual, agency, and network). They found that networks that were highly centralized around a single core actor who coordinated service provision and delivery were the most effective. Thus, the core actor was the focal point around which mental health services were coordinated throughout the community (Provan and Milward, 1995).

Similarly, the DDD network was extremely cohesive in terms of its density and centralization, but essentially did not have one focal actor who coordinated information and resource flow within the project. Rather, the network had five core actors who saw themselves as participants in a project but also as independent entities. Implementation sites mitigated certain kinds of information and resource flow among the network and thus were ineffective and unable to share best practices with one another.

Another factor at play in the DDD network was the type of relation measured within the egocentric networks. Actors can be related through many types of ties and relations. Thus, ties could include social roles, kinship, actions, transfer or flows of resources, or co-occurrence. So two individuals can be neighbors, they can like or dislike each other, they may or may not socialize together, or they may or may not belong to similar associations. When network data are collected, they are generally sampled from among a set of relations, and actors and networks can have multiple relations.

In the DDD network, ties were measured for existence or absence, strength, and value. This type of data collection was limited to those who were involved in the evaluation of the demonstration program because they were the most knowledgeable regarding the program and its operations. In addition, these were the individuals who would provide the most valid information regarding the network study in comparison to the evaluation of the DDD program. Thus, data were focused on single relations between actors and only those relations that were involved within the program under study. Access to data and actors beyond the purview of the evaluation was limited. Data collection is often constrained by the context of the evaluation, so evaluators must make do with the information provided. This could lead to the collection of only single relational data among actors and potentially lead to limited network analyses. Nevertheless, single relational data can still provide valuable insights into program structure, function, resource and information flow, and policy implications.

In the DDD network it appeared that the affiliation sites shared routine information among one another but not individual information. Thus, they shared information such as meeting times, federal and state mandates and policies, and newsletters but not operational, functional, and clinical information. Again, this is often the case with multisite evaluations as implementation sites view each other as separate and distinct entities within the larger context of a program. It is true that each site is often independent of one another, but not so dissimilar in how it provides services that it could not share operational information. Yet implementation sites often do not reveal more individual information, perhaps due to the desire to maintain their sphere of power and resources. As noted, the information asymmetry among the DDD network core actors allowed them to maintain control and position over the other actors in the network. In the case of INC, it exhibited the largest egocentric network and had greater depth and numbers of relations across local, state, and federal environments within the network. This allowed INC to take advantage of resources within and outside its network, which benefited its consumers through the provision of more individualized services, a factor in increased consumer outcomes.

As noted by an employee in the staff survey who suggested that management create a list of community resources for consumers, identifying network linkages can aid in organizational performance. If the evaluation team had looked at this from a network perspective, the questions asked of staff would have focused on process in a more global sense. Questions would have centered on whom the agencies interacted with and the type, quality, and quantity of those relationships. The differences in the INC network could have prompted further investigation into the structure of that implementation site, and differences in program structures among sites would have been discovered much earlier than the fourth year of the project. It also could have allowed understanding of the nature of such a closely knit network and encouraged discussion regarding open communication among implementation sites. Instead of the density and centralization of the network inhibiting information and resource flow, it could have been a conduit for diffusion of ideas and best practices to provide better outcomes.

References

Brass, D. J., Galaskiewicz, J., Greve, H. R., and Tsai, W. "Taking Stock of Networks and Organizations: A Multilevel Perspective. *Academy of Management Journal,* 2004, *47,* 795–817.

Burt, R. S. *Structural Holes: The Social Structure of Competition.* Cambridge, Mass.: Harvard University Press, 1992.

Burt, R. S. "The Contingent Value of Social Capital." *Administrative Science Quarterly,* 1997, *42,* 339–364.

Coleman, J. S. "Social Capital in the Creation of Human Capital." *American Journal of Sociology,* 1988, *94,* S95–S120.

Flood, R. L. *Rethinking the Fifth Discipline.* New York: Routledge, 1999.

Frank, K. "Identifying Cohesive Subgroups." *Social Networks,* 1995, *17,* 27–56.

Kilduff, M., and Tsai, W. *Social Networks and Organizations.* Thousand Oaks, Calif.: Sage, 2003.

Marsden, P. V. "Network Data and Measurement." *American Review of Sociology,* 1990, *16,* 435–463.

Marsden, P. V. "Social Networks." In E. F. Borgatta and R.J.V. Montgomery (eds.), *Encyclopedia of Sociology.* (2nd ed.) New York: Macmillan, 2000.

Monge, P. R., and Contractor, N. S. *Theories of Communication Networks.* New York: Oxford University Press, 2003.

Podolny, J. M., and Baron, J. M. "Resources and Relationships: Social Networks and Mobility in the Workplace." *American Sociological Review,* 1997, *62,* 673–693.

Provan, K. G., and Milward, H. B. "A Preliminary Theory of Interorganizational Network Effectiveness: A Comparative Study of Four Community Mental Health Systems." *Administrative Sciences Quarterly,* 1995, *40,* 1–33.

Wasserman, S., and Faust, K. *Social Network Analysis: Methods and Applications.* Cambridge: Cambridge University Press, 1994.

KIMBERLY A. FREDERICKS is assistant professor of public administration and policy in the Department of Political Science, Indiana State University.

New Directions for Evaluation • DOI 10.1002/ev

6

This chapter describes the application of social network analysis to evaluate the knowledge capacity of a business initiative program at a government-owned national laboratory.

Application of Network Analysis in Evaluating Knowledge Capacity

Sandra M. Birk

This chapter presents the findings from a network analysis conducted to assess the individual and collective knowledge necessary for the Hydrogen Initiative Program at the government-owned Idaho National Laboratory to be successful. The aim of this chapter is to describe a social network analysis (SNA) application by providing a framework for its use in a process-based program evaluation to assess knowledge capacity. This case study involved surveying all thirty-eight program members who were working on the hydrogen initiative, using SNA to analyze the survey results, and then asking a focus group of staff members to explain and comment on the network analysis results. Three general indicators were used to assess the knowledge capacity of the Hydrogen Initiative Program: expert selection, frequency of selection, and connectedness.

Background of the Hydrogen Initiative Program

The Idaho National Laboratory has had several research and development projects since the 1990s to examine the production, storage, and distribution of hydrogen as an alternate fuel source. In 2004 the laboratory consolidated these projects into the Hydrogen Initiative Program, identified the initiative as a major business line for the laboratory, and brought in a manager from outside the laboratory to lead the initiative. This appointment did not imply the traditional organizational structure where all individuals working within the initiative report directly to the manager and reside in the

New Directions for Evaluation, no. 107, Fall 2005 © Wiley Periodicals, Inc.
Published online in Wiley InterScience (www.interscience.wiley.com) • DOI: 10.1002/ev.162

same general location. Rather, each of the thirty-eight employees working on the initiative reported directly to different home organization managers, and they were located in various buildings and locations, with some as far as thirty miles apart. Due to the breadth of skills necessary for the initiative, laboratory management envisioned a cross-cutting project structure that allowed members of the initiative to cross departmental boundaries to access the expertise required for their individual efforts.

No outcome or process-based evaluations had been completed in the short time the program had existed before this evaluation was conducted. As an emerging business initiative that was making the transition from several individual research and development projects into a business line for the laboratory, the newly appointed manager expressed interest in assessing the individual and collective knowledge skills available within the initiative. Companies have lamented the need to understand what they know as an organization, who knows it, where it resides, and how it is communicated to members (O'Dell and Grayson, 1998). Others have suggested that industry and business leaders need tools to make knowledge capacity visible (Holtshouse, 1998; Rulke, Zaheer, and Anderson, 2000). Although the program manager did not express these concerns or have an immediate decision that required results from this evaluation, he was interested in understanding the knowledge capacity of the initiative program and the use of SNA to reveal that capability. However, by knowing who staff perceived as the initiative experts, where they were, and how individuals were connected to each other, the manager would have evaluative data that could help him make future decisions about organizational structure, retention, hiring, or succession planning.

Evaluation Overview

This evaluation was designed to answer four major questions:

1. Who are the experts as perceived by the members of the initiative in each of forty-seven knowledge areas? (Is there more than one expert? Do perceived experts have more years of service than others? Are some perceived to be more valuable than others?)
2. Can we tell which members are in a position to control information flow within the initiative by looking at expert selection?
3. Can we tell how well connected the initiative is by looking at expert selection?
4. What affects the selection of experts?

Although many program evaluations are focused on evaluating overall success or failure of a program to accomplish its goal, the Hydrogen Initiative Program was too new to make such a determination. McNamara (1998) defines program evaluation as "collecting information about a program or one aspect of a program in order to make necessary decisions about the program." In this case, a process-based evaluation that focused on one aspect of the program, knowledge capacity, was appropriate to gain a better understanding of what knowledge resources and expertise were available for program members to access. The methods to answer the evaluation questions included a series of semistructured interviews and an e-mail survey.

The evaluation was designed in three phases. Through e-mails and interviews, a focus group of technical leads in the program developed a single list of knowledge categories or topics required by the initiative to be successful as a business venture. Normally assessment is compared against a standard set of criteria. In this case, there was no worldwide, national, or even local industry consensus of knowledge for hydrogen research. Therefore, it was necessary to establish that benchmark set of knowledge based on the expertise of the initiative's management team. The manager of the initiative reviewed and approved the final list. The intent of this phase was to develop the categories of knowledge and place them within a template question format in an e-mail survey, including items such as, "From whom would you seek advice and information in the area of —?" This approach to SNA was modeled after studies by Durland (2003), Granovetter (1995), and Krebs (1998).

In phase 2, a survey of the network of hydrogen initiative engineers, modeled after the work of Anklam (2002), Krackhardt (1987), and Krebs, Logan, and Zhelka (2001), identified those individuals whom engineers sought for advice and information in each of the forty-seven knowledge categories (questions). Engineers were asked to select one name from a pick list provided for each question or provide a name if their selection was not on the list. The thirty-eight program members selected among themselves and also identified an additional fifty-nine individuals outside the program as expert sources of knowledge, making a ninety-seven-member total network of expertise for the program, as well as forty-seven individual networks, one for each area of knowledge.

E-mail responses for each individual were compiled into spreadsheets that recorded selections of experts in each knowledge area. The spreadsheets were loaded into an SNA software package, UCINET6, for analysis, and the results were delivered to NetDraw, a software package that created the graphical representations of the networks for each question. SNA was used as the primary data analysis tool because the results provide a visualization of the group's knowledge and relationships in a concrete and easy-to-understand form. It allows one to "see the forest and the trees and how they are related" (Krebs, 1998). In addition, the images can help communicate the network structure to end users (Speel and others, 1999).

In phase 3, I met individually with focus group members to explore and further describe findings from the SNA (Creswell, 2003; Tashakkori

Figure 6.1. Knowledge Area with Clearly Identified Expert

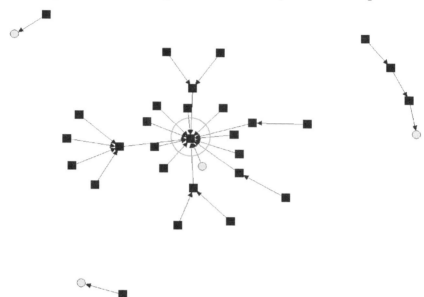

Note: The node within the circle has the largest indegree. Squares are program managers, circles are outside experts.

and Teddlie, 1998). Anklam (2004) recommends follow-up interviews after data analysis to "ensure that the data are positioned in the context of the organization and will not be misinterpreted or misused." Focus group members examined the statistical results and provided their insights regarding data accuracy. They also examined sociograms for each knowledge category and provided their explanation and reasoning for the connections among members of the hydrogen initiative.

Summary of Results

Because "the unit of analysis in network analysis is not the individual, but an entity consisting of a collection of individuals and the linkages among them" (Wasserman and Faust, 1994, p. 5), one cannot use traditional statistics and data analysis measures. Therefore, an entire body of measures has been developed for analysis of the relationships at the individual actor, subgroup, and network level. Some of these measures were selected to analyze the survey data. In Figures 6.1 and 6.2, centrality indegree was used as the measure and to construct the sociograms. Figure 6.3 was constructed from

Figure 6.2. Knowledge Area with Unclear Expert Identification

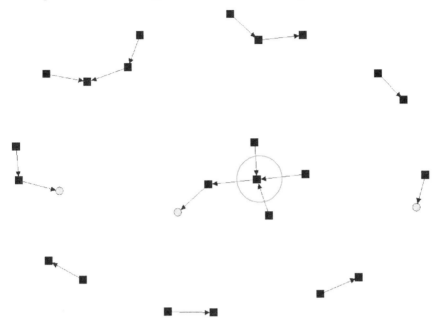

Note: The node within the circle has the largest indegree.

Figure 6.3. Experts Most Central to the Program

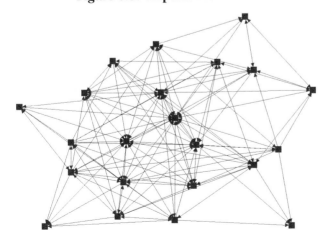

the data of the most central experts across all forty-seven networks, as measured by centrality indegree.

The patterns of identification indicated that the members of the Hydrogen Initiative Program were fairly aware of the knowledge capability for the program. Centrality measures (indegree and betweenness) identified experts in each of the forty-seven knowledge areas. In some cases, the expert was clearly identified, as shown in Figure 6.1. Figure 6.2 shows that for other questions, the expert was not as obvious, and the selections of experts were scattered among many clusters and even single individuals. Approximately half of the questions resulted in maps that clearly identified an expert.

In phase 3, team members confirmed clearly identified experts and offered explanations for those questions that lacked an obvious expert. Members offered that the area of expertise indicated by a question had not advanced to a state that required the knowledge detailed in a question and therefore they were unaware of any experts. In other areas, some members suggested that expertise did not exist and individual selections were merely assumptions that the individual selected might know an expert in the area. Network centrality measures were used to identify eight experts who were critical to the overall network, such that if they left, there would be a clear void. These individuals were easily identified: they had the most connections in the graphical representation of all the expert selections made by team members for all forty-seven questions, as shown in Figure 6.3. Of all the experts identified, interviews in phase 3 revealed that generally the experts did not have more years of experience than others in the program. In fact, the highest-scoring experts placed midrange in the total years of service of all program members.

Betweenness measures showed that some individuals were better positioned in the network to control information flow than others. This means that they would be in a position that required others seeking expertise to go through them first. Many knowledge areas showed individuals in positions of betweenness (see Figure 6.4). However, these positions did not appear on sociograms for the network when compared across all knowledge areas, as shown in Figure 6.5. Therefore it was concluded that no individual, through expert identification, was placed in a strong position to control the flow of information. In this case, the identification of other experts between individuals was possible because team members could access alternate routes to seek expertise.

Network depictions of each knowledge area did not show that the initiative members were well connected to each other. In some cases, the network members were highly dispersed, as shown in Figure 6.2. However, the value of SNA is that it allows multiple views of data to understand a program. By examining the connections among the highest-scoring experts across all knowledge areas, as shown in Figure 6.3, one can observe that the highest-scoring experts are well connected to each other, and therefore one

Figure 6.4. Individuals in Positions of Betweenness

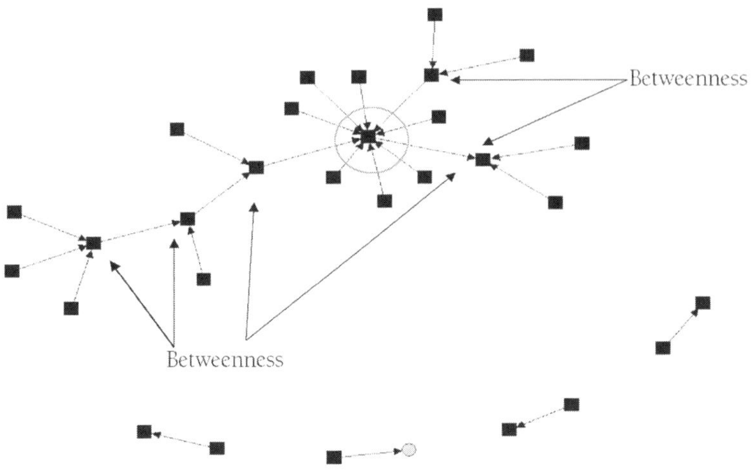

Note: The node within the circle has the largest indegree.

could assume that others who accessed one of these experts would have a pathway to other experts in the network. In addition, ego networks or the network of all connections to an individual, such as the one shown in Figure 6.6, revealed that the highest-scoring experts were well connected with members of the team, and presumably other members could easily reach an expert through these paths of the highest-scoring ego.

Figure 6.5. Betweenness Roles

Figure 6.6. Ego Map

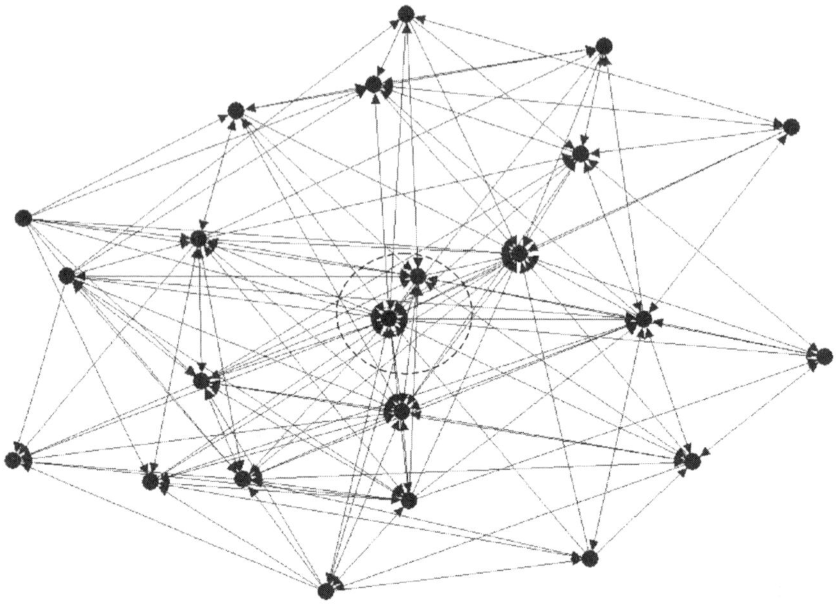

Note: Ego is individual in bottom left of circle.

Discussion

The graphical representations or network maps from SNA provide an excellent starting point for discussions about project capacity. The maps inspired discussion with little prompting, and program members often offered explanations for the selections. Phase 3 revealed several factors that influenced the selection of individuals as sources of expertise: technical specialty, assigned project, proximity to others, and affiliation with the same organizational department.

SNA often reveals more information that helps to depict the real story of a program. Results of the network analysis also revealed the roles that individuals played in the program. Central connectors (Cross, Parker, and Borgatti, 2002; Krebs, 1998) were the highest-scoring experts and linked most of the employees in the network. The loss of these individuals could create a void in the program, and phase 3 interviews frequently cited the value of these individuals and expressed concern over their potential loss to retirement or other companies. Ego maps revealed boundary spanners: those who accessed expertise outside the program (Hargadon, 1998). Several individuals were boundary spanners and well positioned to contribute new ideas and perspectives from outside the team for problem solving and innovation (Hargadon, 1998). Peripheral specialists (Cross, 2004) were easily visible on the maps for each knowledge area. These individuals had some specialized expertise and worked apart from most others in the program. Program members readily recognized these individuals in the network maps and offered explanations suggesting that the project was the driving reason for the lack of connection because the work did not require interaction with others in the program. These individuals were most likely to leave a program because they were isolated from the work team (Krebs, 2002), so management was encouraged to find other ways to have them interact with the team.

Finally, information brokers were those who appeared to play roles of betweenness as they provided a link between groups of individuals (Zack, 2000). These individuals were readily observed in the network maps for each knowledge area and were generally managers who facilitated connections between individuals and sources of expertise.

Conclusions

Anklam (2004) recommends interviews after social network data analysis. However, this recommendation appears to be more of a casual recommendation than a serious commitment. The evaluation described in this case study concluded that interviews with a representative set of individuals from the group under evaluation are essential and even mandatory to ensure that conclusions drawn from the data are accurate and explainable. Even when a deliberate effort is made to obtain feedback, the results should be used discreetly and with caution, especially in areas where the data are not fully explained or where maintaining the anonymity of the participants is desirable.

SNA is a good tool to characterize expertise and capture the connections between individuals and their sources of experts because it makes the unseen and unknown visible and concrete. It is especially valuable for programs where all individuals do not reside within the same organizational department or location. It is also helpful to managers who may not have time to investigate all the potential areas of expertise required for their business initiatives. It provides a systematic way to quickly understand the knowledge capacity of a group. The resulting sociograms clearly highlight business-relevant features and positions occupied by individuals in the program in easy-to-understand pictures of the network structure (Speel and others, 1999). Managers are able to see at a glance those whom the program depends on and how much. As Patton (2005) notes, SNA can reveal who program experts are and who may be bottlenecks because too many people go to them, identify experts who are close to retirement, and make the lack of necessary connections between individuals within a program painfully clear.

SNA measurements allow examination of data from multiple views to ensure a fuller understanding of the results. This is attractive as one can review the quantitative raw data sets, tables of quantitative network analysis measures, or the suite of visual maps that represent the network. The results from such an evaluation are time and context sensitive. No one can be sure that as individual projects within the initiative program move to the next phase, the program begins to integrate staff, or the program expands as rapidly as anticipated, that the results would be the same even in the near future. How rapidly the changes might occur to the network structure is unknown and likely varies with the stability of the program under study.

Limitations

For a novice evaluator, SNA is complex and difficult to complete without support. As noted in Chapter One, individuals who use SNA in evaluation must be proficient at choosing and using a software package for SNA. In addition, they must have the standard skill set for developing questions for surveys and aligning network measures to evaluation questions. Training courses are available from numerous private entities and universities. But perhaps a better way to learn to apply SNA is to begin the process and hire a consultant who is proficient in the software to reduce evaluation data. In addition, if e-mail is the mechanism for collecting survey data, evaluators must have expertise or access to those familiar with electronic systems that collect and tabulate data automatically and safeguard those data on private servers.

One could argue that identification of experts who demonstrate a program's knowledge capacity could be more readily obtained through a few key informants. In fact, during this study, one program member made this suggestion. However, a single individual speaks from personal intuition and a single ego perspective. That individual would not have the perspective of the entire program in all knowledge areas and would not be able to identify who is relied on as an expert, how much, and in what areas. In addition, it is doubtful that even a few key informants would be able to explain the connections and paths individuals take to seek expertise beyond those they themselves know, or in other words, from their own egonet. Finally, a few key informants cannot provide a program perspective, justify and defend their views with hard quantitative data, and provide that information in an easy-to-understand format in a way that SNA can.

References

Anklam, P. "Social Network Analysis." Slides presented at KMWorld Conference, Santa Clara, Calif., Oct. 2002. Retrieved Mar. 21, 2004, from http://www.byeday.net/sna/.
Anklam, P. "About Social Network Analysis for Knowledge Management." 2004. Retrieved Mar. 21, 2004, from http://www.byeday.net/sna/.
Creswell, J. Research Design: Qualitative, Quantitative, and Mixed Methods Approaches. (2nd ed.) Thousand Oaks, Calif.: Sage, 2003.
Cross, R. Interpreting a Network Diagram. 2004. Retrieved Mar. 9, 2004, from http://gates.comm.virginia.edu/rlc32/htm.

Cross, R., Parker, A., and Borgatti, S. *A Bird's Eye View: Using Social Network Analysis to Improve Knowledge Creation and Sharing.* Somers, N.Y.: IBM Corporation, 2002.

Durland, M. "Report on the Network Structures and Characteristics of the Hill Side Business: A Sample Sociometric Technical Report." DeKalb, Ill.: Durland Consulting, 2003.

Granovetter, M. *Getting a Job: A Study in Contacts and Careers.* (2nd ed.) Chicago: University of Chicago Press, 1995.

Hargadon, A. "Firms as Knowledge Brokers: Lessons in Pursuing Continuous Innovation." *California Management Review,* 1998, *40*(3), 209–227.

Holtshouse, D. "Knowledge Research Issues." *California Management Review,* 1998, *40*(3), 277–280.

Krackhardt, D. "Cognitive Social Structures." *Social Networks,* 1987, *9,* 109–134.

Krebs, V. *Knowledge Networks: Mapping and Measuring Knowledge Creation, Reuse, and Flow.* 1998. Retrieved Aug. 12, 2004, from http://www.orgnet.com/IHRIM.html.

Krebs, V. *InFlow 3.0 Network Mapping Software.* 2002. Retrieved Aug. 16, 2004, from http://www.orgnet.com/inflow3.html.

Krebs, V., Logan, M., and Zhelka, E. "Tacit and Explicit: Measure and Map It." Paper presented at KMWorld 2001, Santa Clara, Calif., Oct. 31, 2001. Retrieved Apr. 7, 2004, from www.infotoday.com/kmw01/presentations/default.htm.

McNamara, C. *Basic Guide to Program Evaluation.* Feb. 16, 1998. Retrieved June 18, 2005, from http://222.mapnp.org/library/evaluation/fnl_eval.htm.

O'Dell, C., and Grayson, J. "If Only We Knew What We Know: Identification and Transfer of Internal Best Practices." *California Management Review,* 1998, *40*(3), 154–174.

Patton, S. "Who Knows Whom, and Who Knows What." *CIO Magazine,* June 15, 2005. Retrieved Oct. 26, 2005, from http://www.cio.com/archive/061505/km.html.

Rulke, D., Zaheer, S., and Anderson, M. "Sources of Managers' Knowledge of Organizational Capabilities." *Organizational Behavior and Human Decision Processes,* 2000, *82*(1), 34–149.

Speel, P., and others. "Knowledge Mapping for Industrial Purposes." In *Proceedings of the KAW'99 Twelfth Workshop on Knowledge Acquisition, Modeling and Management,* Banff, Alberta, Canada, Oct. 1999. Retrieved May 10, 2004, from http://sern.ucalgary.ca/KSI/KAW/KAW99/papers/Speel1/index.html.

Tashakkori, A., and Teddlie, C. *Mixed Methodology: Combining Qualitative and Quantitative Approaches.* Thousand Oaks, Calif.: Sage, 1998.

Wasserman, S., and Faust, K. *Social Network Analysis: Methods and Applications.* Cambridge: Cambridge University Press, 1994.

Zack, M. "Researching Organizational Systems Using Social Network Analysis." In *Proceedings of the 33rd Hawaii International Conference on Systems Sciences.* Maui, Hawaii, Jan. 2000. IEEE Los Alamitos, Calif.: Computer Society Press, 2000. Retrieved May 10, 2004, from http://web.cba.neu.edu/~mzack/articles/socnet/socnet.htm.

SANDRA M. BIRK is program manager for Battelle Energy Alliance at the Idaho National Laboratory. Her case study was based on her dissertation, for which she received the Outstanding Dissertation Award from the University of Idaho and the Life Long Learning Association.

7

*This chapter's case was a formative evaluation to guide
the effectiveness and efficiency of a planned integration.
The system network analysis application is illustrative of
organizational structures.*

A Formative Evaluation of the
Integration of Two Departments

Maryann M. Durland

This case describes the evaluation of the integration of two departments in
a large firm in the Midwest. The integration process, implemented through
the office of the director and selected senior managers, was initiated as part
of a larger reorganization strategy that included eliminating duplication in
services, offering new client services, and eliminating less productive service areas. Following processes outlined within an organization-wide strategic plan, its goal was to merge two distinct groups into one operating unit
with little or no noticeable disruption of service to clients. The two groups,
totaling about 250 employees, provided services to the larger organization
of over ten thousand employees. These distinct groups had some overlap of
focus and services and complementary structures and knowledge areas, but
some areas of difference. Through the integration process, they needed to
become one unit.

Background

Prior to and during the merger process, department heads had spent extensive time on strategic planning and preparation. The integration included
eliminating, creating, and renaming knowledge areas. Knowledge areas represented content or services (leadership training, curriculum and instructional design, assessment development, program evaluation, information
technology, online survey development, and team development, for example). The planning and preparation included initiatives for establishing new

NEW DIRECTIONS FOR EVALUATION, no. 107, Fall 2005   © Wiley Periodicals, Inc.
Published online in Wiley InterScience (www.interscience.wiley.com) • DOI: 10.1002/ev.163

relationships while using existing relationships within and across departments. The integration was implemented in stages and included information and activities that clarified the new vision of organization structure and the processes and procedures available to build integrated work groups and establish new communication structures. Each department already applied a business model of work groups and teaming to meet service area goals. Establishing new relationships across the integrated department would form a larger matrix for staffing work groups on specific project specifications. This larger matrix would provide access to more knowledge areas than one department had alone, although each department had had limited contact with the other in the course of meeting very specialized staffing needs on a few previous projects.

Evaluation Goals. The formative evaluation was designed to address two key goals: documenting the process and progress toward the integration of the two departments and identifying the structural characteristics of the interactions between and among the members of the two previous departments to further a successful integration process. Network analysis was identified as a methodology that could facilitate the merger process through measures aligned to the conceptualized structural characteristics of the merger (integrated work teams and so on). SNA could facilitate the merger in three ways: (1) identifying problem issues or areas that needed to be immediately addressed, thereby increasing the effectiveness of the integration process; (2) having information about the progress of the integration during the process rather than when a significant problem was suspected in retrospect (then researching the history to locate when, where, and why a problem existed), thereby increasing the efficiency of the integration process; and (3) benchmarking the process of integration for future reference.

Informal Communication. This evaluation focused on informal links, which are different from formal links, defined by organization charts, personnel classification, and assignments (McPhee and Tompkins, 1985). Informal links are the communication patterns defined by work relationships (Cross and Parker, 2004). They may align with formal project assignments, but that correspondence was not the underlying interest in this evaluation. Formal project assignments could be measured by tracking work group staffing classified by organizational chart classifications. The main focus of this evaluation was first to determine to what degree the two departments had integrated to the extent that they could be identified as one through the informal work links (in other words, by the ways in which work was done) and, second, to pinpoint areas of strength and weakness to inform further strategic planning. The evaluation was conducted early in the integration process, about four months after it was formally put into practice, but after enough time had passed so that there had been opportunities for establishing new relationships and there was a sense of stability.

NEW DIRECTIONS FOR EVALUATION • DOI 10.1002/ev

The relationship focus was on the informal links, given that during change such as this integration, the major goal of implementation processes, strategies, and activities is to move group members' understanding and perception of the organization from an existing formal structure to a new formal structure, that is, in this evaluation, a new structure created by the integration of two departments. During this change process, the existing informal communication structures, interaction paths, established communication patterns, and prior cross-teaming experiences would also need to change or integrate into the new structure. Informal structures do not change automatically based on changes in the formal structure (Cross and Parker, 2004). Informal structures indicate what works and what is comfortable, and were considered to be the primary indicators of structural change.

Network analysis would provide images of the current state and validate the projected integrated model, described below. The premise for targeting informal communication was that during change processes, some level of fear or discomfort is generally associated with the "place in between" the old and new. From a structural perspective, this place in between can translate into a feeling or perception of disjointedness, or not knowing what was going on, as individuals move among the three structural elements: the new formal organizational structures, the existing formal structures, and the existing informal structures. (In preintegration focus groups, qualitative data verified this feeling of disjointedness.) The formative evaluation was designed to discover if structural characteristics could distinguish this place in between and thereby focus resources for moving toward the new structure. Aligning the model with specific structural characteristics would be a way to measure the level of disjointedness and the integration experience of moving from one formal structure to another through the lens of the informal links.

Development of the Projected Structural Model of Integration. This evaluation focused on answering the question, "What are the structural characteristics that define the process and look of integrating two distinct organizational units into one?" Given the design of the new organization and its operating characteristics, two areas were identified as illustrative of the proposed new organizational structure: team characteristics and overall network patterns and leadership characteristics. *Team* was defined as meaning the new department, and smaller work groups were within the larger team structure.

A two-step process was used to create the model. First, the qualitative characteristics and indicators of a successfully integrated organization, according to the business model supporting the integration, were identified, and then these characteristics and indicators were aligned with corresponding structural features that could be measured with SNA. The model in essence moved from a verbalization of integration to a visualization. Qualitative features relevant to the integration were identified and defined from numerous sources, including organizational documents, documents resulting from the work of the formal transition and integration teams, integration activities, and discussions with directors and managers. A projected model can provide a set of guidelines by which to evaluate the evolving integration structure. A model can also portray an image of the envisioned integrated organization that can be used as a benchmarking and diagnostic tool. In addition, a model with aligned SNA indicators can be a method for establishing a visual focus by which to build common understanding of the current and future states of an organization in the process of change.

Second, and more broadly, the evaluation investigated how management could use a model for understanding one aspect of systemic, organizational change that would be applicable to the implementation of future innovations. SNA images provided an approach for locating characteristics of structure as visualized in the model and of potential disjointedness, thus triangulating with other observations and measures of perceptions. The team and overall network and leadership patterns were theorized to have specific structural characteristics if the integration process was implemented and working as the strategic planning had defined.

Integration Model

The model for the integration of the two teams provided the framework for identifying the communication components and network characteristics that would be measured. Two areas are described here: first, the total team and overall network of the two departments, and second, the position of leadership, both formally defined and informally identified within the new structure.

Team and Overall Network. A successful integration would include members well connected within work groups, members connected in multiple ways across work groups (measured by degree and cliques), and a well-defined overall team structure formed by the underlying pattern of the connections of the work groups (such as multiple overlapping cliques), indicating a teaming structure. The new team would form a clearly defined, overall webbed or well-connected structure.

Leadership. The success of the integration process was modeled as having top leadership clearly connected within the overall team structure and top leadership clearly central to both integrated departments. In network terms, the structure would be a dense network with few isolates, and the communication paths would be well connected with only one network component.

Evaluation Design

Two questions were asked in an online survey. Respondents were first asked to select those individuals with whom they had had communication since the date of the formal integration, with all members of each department included in a forced-choice list. Communication was defined as any communication content other than social in nature. It could be face-to-face, telephone contact, telephone message, or e-mail. A second question asked the respondent to list the three individuals with whom they had had the most work-related contact since the integration. The survey was sent by an e-mail link to 213 individuals; 174 individuals responded, for an 82 percent response rate. All 213 individuals were included in creating the networks for the analysis, as some analyses disregarded the direction of the tie, and other analyses such as the mutual pairs excluded individuals if they were an isolate. The definition of the network and whether to include nonrespondents is a reoccurring issue in doing SNA (Richards, 1985; Laumann, Marsden, and Prensky, 1989; Breiger, 1991; Wasserman and Faust, 1994).

Network Definition. Twelve networks created from the data collected were used in the investigation. The twelve networks encompassed four networks constructed with the members of the combined new department and four networks constructed with the members of each of the two departments separately. Each set of four networks included the total network, which was all of the communication pairs regardless of direction (from one individual or both) created from the first question; the mutual network, which was the reciprocated communication pairs created from the first network; the top three choices network; and the top three choices mutual network. To create the mutual networks, the total networks were constructed, and then a second network was constructed that transformed the mutual choices to 1 and all other choices to 0 (Borgatti, Everett, and Freeman, 1992).

The networks for each old department were constructed from extracting the data from the total network so that each old department had a total network, a mutual network, a top three network, and a top three mutual network. Only the results for the combined team are reported here.

Communication Levels. Each of the subsequent networks in the set of four illustrates the four levels of communication defined for this evaluation; each subsequent network in a set of four increases the restrictions on the strength of the communication between any two individuals. In the total network, the relationship is nondirectional, meaning that only one individual need indicate the relationship. In this network, the choices are binary; communication exists or does not. This communication link is then restricted in the mutual network to count as a communication if a link is reciprocated or if both individuals agreed. In the third and fourth networks, the data are limited to the top three choices respondents indicated they communicated with, again restricted in the fourth network to reciprocated links. Table 7.1 provides an example of the matrices for each of the networks and what the data would look like.

Creating mutual networks (reciprocated ties) is a two-step process. First, the valued networks are transformed to binary values. Second, the

Table 7.1. Example Matrices

	Total Network						Mutual Network			
	A	B	C	D	E		A	B	C	D	E
A	0	1	4	2	0	A	0	1	1	1	0
B	3	0	4	1	2	B	1	0	1	1	1
C	4	0	0	0	0	C	1	0	0	0	0
D	1	1	0	0	1	D	1	1	0	0	1
E	4	3	2	1	0	E	0	1	1	1	0
	Total 1,2,3 Network						Mutual 1,2,3 Network			
	A	B	C	D	E		A	B	C	D	E
A	0	0	4	2	0	A	0	0	1	1	0
B	3	0	4	0	2	B	0	0	1	0	1
C	4	0	0	0	0	C	1	0	0	0	0
D	0	0	0	0	0	D	0	0	0	0	0
E	4	3	2	0	0	E	0	1	0	0	0

mutual ties are selected. As a result, in the mutual networks, the reciprocated links are not based on the original value of the relationship. For example, person A picked person B as his or her last choice, and person B picked person A as his or her second choice. (Reverse values are used for rankings, so that first choice has a value of 4, second choice a value of 3, third choice a value of 2, and selected, no ranking, a value of 1.)

Communication was the term used in this survey because of the nature of the work of these departments (Rogers and Kincaid, 1981). It would be expected that members of a work group would have frequent communication about a project and that a variety of tools would be used. It was common for both departments to leave broadcast voice messages for all members of the work group, to meet face to face, and to follow up with e-mail. It was also common and expected that individuals would be members of several work groups and that work groups could have a diverse combination of members depending on the skill sets needed for the project.

These restrictions provided levels of communication that were established to provide the broadest to the narrowest estimates of structure. The range of network views, from broadest to narrowest communication, created a framework for understanding the change process that would allow the inclusion of nonrespondents and establish a best-to-worst case set of indicators. This case summarizes the structural characteristics of the four networks of the integrated team and the accompanying network measures that were calculated. Two specific measures, components and cliques, will be discussed.

NEW DIRECTIONS FOR EVALUATION • DOI 10.1002/ev

Analysis

The analysis of the data included looking at the total network and how well connected it was overall, then at how well the integration had occurred between the two teams. As the analysis led to identifying specific patterns, cliques were chosen as a measure to explore and explain some of the overall patterns and to further identify underlying patterns in the structure. The next sections describe these two areas of analysis.

Components. Components are a measure of the number of breaks in a network. They indicate the connectedness of a network to the extent that there is a path to all of the individuals within a component and there is no link to anyone outside the component. A network with one component means that there is a communication path to every individual within that component. As the restrictions on communication were applied and the data in the networks reflected these restrictions, the number of network components increased. Components are a reflection not of the size of the network but of the inclusiveness of communication. With the broadest definition of communication, there was one component for the total network. This means that, disregarding the direction of the communication and in essence allowing every link to represent communication, everyone could be reached on some path. The total mutual network had twenty components. When the communication for the network was reduced to the top three choices, the number of components was five, and the top three/mutual network had 123 components. This change is apparent in the following figures. Figure 7.1 is the sociogram for the total network, constructed from the raw data. Noted in the network are the two teams coded by shape and the mass of lines going throughout the network indicating lines of communication between individuals. No arrows are provided in the sociogram to facilitate seeing the overall patterns. The average amount of communication calculated by indegree (coming from others) and by outdegree (going to others) was about the same.

Team Patterns. Two notable patterns are indicated. First is the top-to-bottom spilt in the network between the two teams; it is clear that although there were lines of communication going back and forth, the two teams had not integrated. Although this sociogram was constructed to accentuate the distinction, the separation was clearly evident. In addition, four loose clusters were noted, which are circled for attention. However, there was only one component. Figure 7.2 is the sociogram for the first, second, and third choices, coded by team. In this sociogram, the arrows have been left on to indicated the direction of the communication. The overall sociogram has an integrated look, though the number of connections is sparse, which indicates less communication overall than expected. The large cluster was one component. The four circles at the top left represented the other four components. Figure 7.3 illustrates the most restrictive definition

Figure 7.1. Total Network for Two Groups

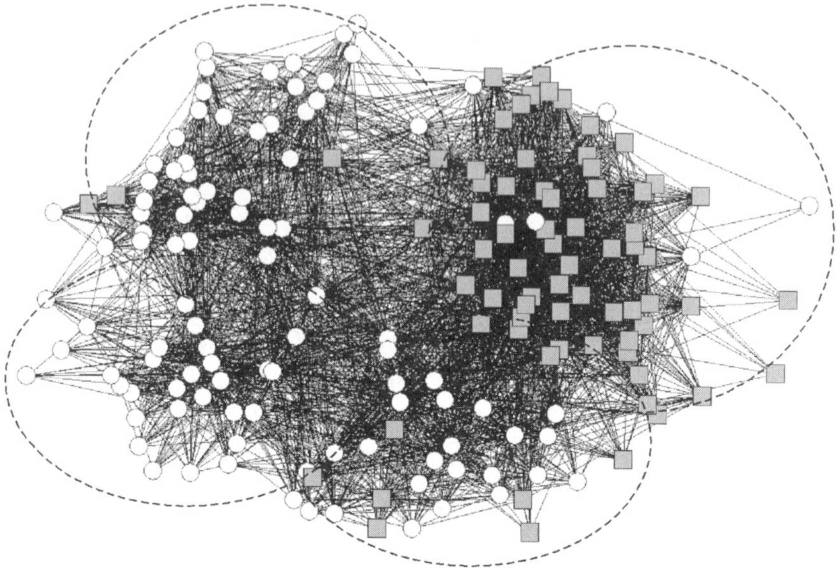

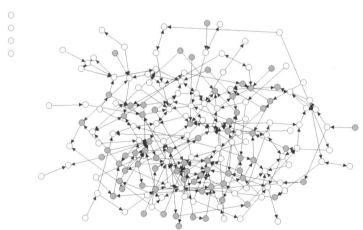

of communication: the mutual network for the first, second, and third top
individuals communicated with.

In Figure 7.3, mutual connections are shown. Each separate set of two
was a component. The isolates are not shown. The change from Figure 7.1
to 7.3 is striking. What this suggested was that although there was activity
on the surface, which would be expected, there was not an underlying

Figure 7.2. Top Three Choices, Coded by Team

Figure 7.3. Top Three Choices: Mutual Network

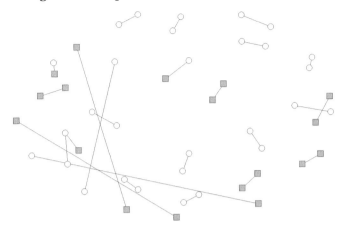

"trusted relationships" structure that interconnected to form a larger group. This was particularly evident in the sociograms. The sociograms in Figures 7.1 to 7.3 illustrate the overall network, viewed with the component information.

Although there were exceptions, the primary connections in these sociograms were within the old department and were one-to-one. There were approximately twenty-five relationships illustrated in Figure 7.3 out of 213 individuals. The percentage of reciprocated ties was 9.27 percent. That there were so few reciprocated ties when there was so much overall activity indicated that individuals may have had one close working relationship, if they had any at all.

One other explanation explored was that with so much project activity (indicated in Figure 7.1), it was possible there was too much going on for any two individuals to form more lasting relationships that would show up in mutual pairs. This might result from the combination of personnel assignments to projects, the skill needs of projects, and the choices individuals made to work on assignments. But given the extent of a project life, which could be anywhere from a month to a year, this did not seem like a plausible explanation. Nor did it seem plausible that individuals did not remember who the top three people were whom they worked with the most.

Cliques. Cliques are small, contained subgroups. Each member of a clique has communication with every other member of the clique. Cliques were calculated beginning with the least restrictive communication definition, meaning that if one individual indicated contact, the communication was counted. Then cliques were determined for each of the networks with more restrictive definitions of communication. Clique analysis began with a traditional clique of three members. Although there were differences in the number of cliques found among the four levels of the networks, because of the construction of the networks, what was most notable was the total number of cliques at the smaller clique sizes and the large twenty-member cliques. There were more than fifty-eight hundred loosely defined cliques of size three (that is, at least three members). Cliques ranged from size three to twenty. "Loosely defined" means that the connection did not have to be mutual. This characterization provided the broadest indicator of communication. The amount of connections indicated that there was a lot of communication activity, with about twenty-seven cliques on average per person (based on 213 individuals in the network). Three individuals were identified as members of over three thousand cliques. There were over a thousand cliques with a minimum size of fifteen members for the total network.

As the definition of communication was restricted for the network, the number of cliques decreased. When the total network was restricted to just the top three choices, the number of cliques was reduced to forty-four of size three. There was only one clique of size four (four members). In the total mutual network there were 927 cliques of minimum size three, 721 of minimum size five, and two of minimum size thirteen.

Leadership Patterns. To understand more about the role of cliques within the network, the cliques identified within the top three choices network were analyzed. Individuals who were members of the forty-four cliques were identified and clustered. In a set of cliques, it would be common for three individuals to be members of clique 1, then two of the three also members of clique 2, with the addition of a new member. This analysis resulted in the co-membership of cliques, and in this team, the co-membership was clustered into two large groups. This meant that of the forty-four cliques, there were actually two large groups of individuals who were the members of those cliques. The location of the members within these two groups that formed the forty-four cliques is illustrated in Figure 7.4. Figure 7.4 was

Figure 7.4. Cliques Within the Restricted Top Three Choices Network

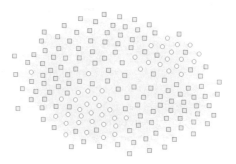

created so that the lines of communication are in the background, and the two clusters of individuals can be seen within the overall network. They are the light-colored circles—one large cluster on the right and one on the bottom left. The squares represent the other members of the two departments. Further analysis of these two cliques indicated that most members were leadership. The pattern confirmed the model that leadership would be central to the total network, but also illustrated that leadership paralleled the overall network and was not as integrated as expected.

Evaluation Summary

The four networks illustrated what appeared to be three distinct kinds of communication activities. The total network seemed to indicate a high level of overall activity, based on the amount of indegreeness and outdegreeness, the components, and the high number of cliques. However, an analysis by old team membership revealed that most communication still took place within these old teams. The mutual network looked similar to the total network, but with reduced connections, so further analysis might explore other levels of the network, based on the location of individuals in the broadest network. These other levels might include all communication excluding the top three.

Three other characteristics were noted. First, there were relatively few isolates in the total network, but isolates increased as the communication definition was restricted. Second, as the number of isolates increased, the network fell apart, so that underneath the entire communication structure as seen in the broadest network, there were actually only a few close relationships. The sharp increase in isolates and the resulting very sparse, "stringy" network occurring together gave the strong suggestion of disjointedness, though no causes or reasons. Third, there were two large clusters made up of the members of the cliques in the top three choices network who seemed to hold the larger network together, although the members were separated into two distinct clusters represented by the old teams. While there appeared to be a lot of overall activity, the old departments had not integrated at the project or the leadership level.

Other findings from the data that are not covered in detail here indicated that top leadership was centrally located within the network on all four sociograms and appeared centrally located within both old departments. On measures of centrality, top leadership was first ranked on the total network and the mutual network, which were theorized to illustrate overall activity and communication structure. Top leadership was not ranked on the most frequent contact network, which supported the theory that this network was project related and the communications were for a different purpose. In addition, for the total network, thirty-three individuals (fewer than 20 percent of the total) held the top ten ranks on the three measures of centrality calculated (normalized indegree, normalized betweenness, and normalized closeness). These individuals corresponded with the clique membership for the two largest clusters.

Conclusion

Network data were used to inform initial questions such as the following: What is the capability for successful integration based on the current communication paths available? What additional links would facilitate attaining integration goals? In management meetings and in informal reports, network data provided answers to these types of questions through the sociograms, sociometric profiles, and the projected model. One of the most important aspects of doing SNA is that the process of analyzing the data and the interpretation of what it means requires client involvement in the discussions. The data analysis can sometimes provide clear directions, such as the information on leadership and the membership of the two large cliques found in this case, but at other times, more information is needed to dig further into the data.

Network analysis is not about the impact of an initiative measured in statistics such as amount of money or number of teams, and it is not a measure of processes, such as how an initiative was implemented and the adherence to an implementation plan, although the results certainly can be used to inform those questions. SNA is about understanding capacity. The informal structure of an organization indicates the capacity for dissemination of information and for the creation of a group culture. Structure illustrates how well members are currently teaming and provides an indication of the level of communication (Mullen, 1987; Rogers, 1975). In addition, with data such as clique membership and centrality measures, management can determine if communication is occurring where it is most useful, if there are any bottlenecks in the flow of communication, and if any individuals need to be more engaged. Formal structures provide a definition of how an organization should look, but the informal interactions indicate how an organization really works (Blau, 1974; Cross and Parker, 2004; Granovetter, 1973; Rogers, 1979). Network analysis methodology provides an efficient and meaningful way to bridge the two structures—one defined on paper, the other existing in practice (Breiger, 1988).

Understanding the structure of organizational systems and knowing where problems are located provides information to address the problems in appropriate ways. For example, areas of low connection may indicate the need to develop formal communication structures or implement improvements to existing communication processes. The overall pattern of connections may also provide details to inform recruiting. The strength and direction of links may indicate models for duplication or, conversely, where links are needed.

Change processes require extensive communication structures. Network analysis provides details on where to target communication and the location of available paths. Assuming that providing information through one channel would not guarantee that the other group would be included, in this case, both of the large clique groups would have to be included in all communications to ensure that everyone got the information. Both of the groups were leadership groups, so finding a way to bridge these groups would be critical to the success of the ultimate integration. During change processes, there is a time span between the initial implementation activities and the expected resulting behavior, activities, and informal structures. Changes to informal structures do not occur in symphony with formal structural changes, and SNA documents that orchestrating change takes a lot more than printing a new organization chart.

References

Blau, P. M. "Parameters of Social Structure." *American Sociological Review*, 1974, *39*, 615–635.

Borgatti, S. P., Everett, M. G., and Freeman L. C. *UCINET IV. Version 1.0 Reference Manual*. Harvard, Mass.: Analytic Technologies, 1992.

Breiger, R. L. "The Duality of Persons and Groups." In B. Wellman and S. D. Berkowitz (eds.), *Social Structures: A Network Approach*. Cambridge: Cambridge University Press, 1988.

Breiger, R. L. *Explorations in Structural Analysis: Dual and Multiple Networks of Social Structure*. New York: Garland Press, 1991.

Cross, R., and Parker, A. *The Hidden Power of Social Networks: Understanding How Work Really Gets Done in Organizations*. Boston: Harvard Business School Press, 2004.

Granovetter, M. "The Strength of Weak Ties." *American Journal of Sociology*, 1973, *78*, 1360–1380.

Laumann, E. O., Marsden, P. V., and Prensky, D. "The Boundary Specification Problem in Network Analysis." In L. C. Freeman, D. R. White, and A. K. Romney (eds.), *Research Methods in Social Network Analysis*. Fairfax, Va.: George Mason University Press, 1989.

McPhee, R. D., and Tompkins, P. K. (eds.). *Organizational Communication: Traditional Themes and New Directions*. Thousand Oaks, Calif.: Sage, 1985.

Mullen, B. "Introduction: The Study of Groups." In B. Mullen and G. Goethals (eds.), *Theories of Group Behavior*. New York: Springer-Verlag, 1987.

Richards, W. D., Jr. "Data, Models, and Assumptions in Network Analysis." In R. D. McPhee and P. K. Tompkins (eds.), *Organizational Communication: Traditional Themes and New Directions*. Thousand Oaks, Calif.: Sage, 1985.

Rogers, E. M. "Network Analysis of the Diffusion of Innovations." In P. W. Holland and S. Leinhardt (eds.), *Perspectives on Social Network Research*. Orlando, Fla.: Academic Press, 1979.

Rogers, E. M., and Kincaid, D. L. *Communication Networks: Toward a New Paradigm for Research*. New York: Macmillan, 1981.

Rogers, R. E. *Organizational Theory*. Needham Heights, Mass.: Allyn & Bacon, 1975.
Wasserman, S., and Faust, K. *Social Network Analysis: Methods and Applications*. Cambridge: Cambridge University Press, 1994.

MARYANN M. DURLAND is an independent consultant specializing in evaluation and in the applications of social network analysis.

NEW DIRECTIONS FOR EVALUATION • DOI 10.1002/ev

8

This chapter frames the use of social network analysis in understanding knowledge diffusion and discusses current uses of this methodology within a government agency.

The Value of Social Network Analysis in Health Care Delivery

David M. Introcaso

In their introduction to this volume, Durland and Fredericks make brief but important mention of complexity. Increased interest in social network analysis (SNA), they say, is due in part to a focus on understanding complex processes. Further discussion of complex responsive or adaptive processes may be helpful as context in understanding the impetus for and utility of SNA, particularly for those interested in using network analysis to evaluate how and why change or innovation happens, or more specifically, for understanding how knowledge or meaning is created and flows. Although there are several (competing) models (Greenhalgh and others, 2004) that attempt to explain innovation (or innovativeness) and spread (or diffusion and dissemination), SNA can always play a role in evaluating program dynamics since networks or relationships are ubiquitous, inherent in any activity.

The traditional paradigm used for understanding information or knowledge exchange is essentially a staged, mechanistic, linear one. How we connect what we know with what we do is defined as a relatively simple staged or sequential communication process whereby information or knowledge is an "it" or a "thing" that can be transferred from one individual to another or one individual receives it from another. From an organizational viewpoint, the issue becomes one of managing information or knowledge assets (explaining the enthusiasm for knowledge management). For example, improving health care delivery (the world in which I work) is largely understood as an effort to provide more research information or communication

NEW DIRECTIONS FOR EVALUATION, no. 107, Fall 2005 © Wiley Periodicals, Inc.
Published online in Wiley InterScience (www.interscience.wiley.com) • DOI: 10.1002/ev.164

infrastructure that facilitates the more rapid transfer or adoption of research findings or clinical evidence (Rogers, 2003).

Complexity suggests, however, that information exchange—or, more accurately, knowledge creation—is a social activity involving much more than merely taking a statement made in one context and mechanistically transferring or reproducing it in another or, as it is sometimes phrased, "dumping it down." Knowledge or knowledge creation, Stacey (2000) has argued, is not simply a sender-receiver communication exercise, where person A transfers to person B. Knowledge arises instead in complex responsive or adaptive processes between human beings. That is, knowledge creation or meaning arises as a "gesture-response." Knowledge is not a thing or a system, but an active process of relating, the property of ongoing relational interaction.

Knowledge in this sense cannot be transferred since it arises (or is continuously reproduced and potentially transformed) out of mutual adaptation between person A and person B. Knowledge or meaning becomes apparent only in the "response" to a "gesture" and therefore lies in the whole or completed social act of gesture-response. Knowledge assets therefore lie in the pattern of relationships between relating beings and are destroyed when those relational patterns are destroyed. In this sense, knowledge or information does not transfer—or transfer is only the partial or incomplete expression of the gesture-response dynamic. In sum, Stacey (2003) argues that complexity suggests an alternative paradigm that is action based, one that emphasizes the social or collaborative nature of the action of talking in which people make sense of their actions together or where knowledge creation is a process of developing shared learning or shared meaning. (What this suggests about human agency is profound: as Stacey has written, the processes of mind are the same processes as social relating or, as sometimes explained, I cannot be me without you.)

With a focus on health care improvement, Wood and Ferlie (2003) have argued that since meaning is not an inherent property of information, health care research should be conducted as a "continuous process of communication" (p. 63), or as argued by Wood, Ferlie, and Fitzgerald (1998), the production of health care knowledge or improvement should be focused on associations across different interest groups and professional fields. The production of research evidence or knowledge does not arise from an independent source. It is not given, preformed or preexistent; neither is its production stable or exogenous. Wood states that knowledge does not proceed discretely from one point to another. Research does not become clinical practice. Instead, there is a becoming from research to practice. Knowledge always inextricably combines with action, interactions, and relationships of practice. Maguire (2002) has argued that the production of research evidence and its translation or adoption (more accurately adaptation) can be simultaneous and entangled. In a study of the process by which treatment innovations for HIV/AIDS became used, Maguire found adoption ultimately depended on several social and communication process variables including usefulness. As the novelist and medical-school-trained Walker Percy (1975, p. 131) wrote, "To a man dying of thirst the news [or knowledge] of diamonds over the next dune is of no significance. But the news of water is."

With knowledge or meaning the product of complex responsive or adaptive processes, the importance or utility of SNA should become readily apparent: network analysis becomes a useful way of making relationships visible, and, once visible or identified, network analysis can be used to develop and support network relationships as well as intentionally create them, all for the purposes of generating shared learning or shared meaning.

The use of SNA tools may be needed in health care delivery due in large part to the long-standing difficulty in increasing the pace at which improvements in clinical practice delivery are made. Numerous Institute of Medicine and other reports demonstrate unacceptable numbers of medical errors, the low percentage of Americans receiving recommended care, and the (literally) generational pace at which research evidence, using Wood's phrase, "becomes practice." In response, the World Health Organization (2005) has recently begun to address this issue, which it defines on its Web site's overview of strategies as the "know-do gap." The National Institutes of Health (NIH) is now attempting to address this issue using its "Roadmap" strategy (http://nihroadmap.nih.gov), which outlines NIH's goal of accelerating or transforming scientific knowledge or research into tangible benefits. Various foundations as well as for-profit organizations are doing similar work. *Health Affairs,* a leading health care policy journal, has recently devoted an entire issue to the topic of producing more health care research or evidence-based medicine and using it faster ("The New Imperative," 2005). (Unfortunately many of these efforts in my opinion assume the "sender-receiver" paradigm.)

My agency, the Agency for Health Care Research and Quality (AHRQ), has several initiatives under way as well to address this issue. AHRQ, an agency of the U.S. Public Health Service within the U.S. Department of Health and Human Services (DHHS), whose mission is to advance health excellence in health care, is evolving from a more strictly limited publishing model of scientific research to include a network model of collaboration. The agency is beginning to improve its own network health or ways in which it can bring people into relation with one another. For example, to improve the quality of care delivered in the United States, the agency this past year announced a new initiative, Quality Connect. Part of this effort will be to create and evaluate, using SNA, a network of hospital chief quality officers. In addition, it has recently networked with nine HMOs and with a few select states to improve diabetes care delivery and associated patient outcomes. AHRQ is as well intentionally working to develop networks and links with partners to address patient safety, disparities in care delivery, and pharmaceutical outcomes. It is networking with other DHHS agencies, for example, the Centers for Medicare and Medicaid Services, and AHRQ is using SNA to create a sampling frame to collect stakeholder input to inform the agency's future research agenda. Furthermore, beyond using network methods to assess these efforts quantitatively and qualitatively, AHRQ is attempting to understand the qualities and capacities of these network interactions—for example, to determine the levels of awareness, concordance, inclusion, intention, respect, trust, and other qualities we are attempting to engender. From a more traditional evaluative perspective, the agency is using network analysis methods to assess the past performance of a number of AHRQ programs. All of these efforts are using or assuming a gesture-response paradigm.

As complexity suggests, programs, innovation, or learning do not proceed in clockwork fashion. Neither should approaches to program evaluation. Complexity suggests that understanding and evaluating programs or systems are contained in the patterns of relationships and interactions among agents in a network.

References

Greenhalgh, T., and others. "Diffusion of Innovations in Service Organizations: Systematic Review and Recommendations." *Milbank Quarterly,* 2004, *82,* 581–630.

Maguire, S. "Discourse and Adoption of Innovations: A Study of HIV/AIDS Treatments." *Health Care Management Review,* 2002, *27,* 74–88.

"The New Imperative: Producing Better Evidence." *Health Affairs,* 2005, *24* (entire issue 1).

Percy, W. *The Message in the Bottle: How Queer Man Is, How Queer Language Is, and What One Has to Do with the Other.* New York: Farrar, Straus and Giroux, 1975.

Rogers, E. *Diffusion of Innovations.* (5th ed.) New York: Free Press, 2003.

Stacey, R. *Complexity and Management: Fad or Radical Challenge to Systems Thinking.* London: Routledge, 2000.

Wood, M., and Ferlie, E. "Journey from Hippocrates with Bergson and Deleuze." *Organization Studies,* 2003, *24*(1), 47–68.

Wood, M., Ferlie, E., and Fitzgerald, L. "Achieving Clinical Behavior Change: A Case of Becoming Indeterminate." *Social Science and Medicine,* 1998, *47,* 1729–1738.

World Health Organization. "Bridging the Know-Do Gap in Global Health." Retrieved 2005 from http://www.who.int/kms/en.

DAVID M. INTROCASO is evaluation officer for the Agency for Healthcare Research and Quality.

This chapter presents some final thoughts about the future of social network analysis within the field of evaluation.

Next Steps for Nodes, Nets, and SNA Analysis in Evaluation

Maryann M. Durland, Kimberly A. Fredericks

Social network analysis (SNA) is not a new methodology, but its application to evaluation practice is new. Ultimately the most important question for evaluation practitioners is: How does SNA add value to evaluation practice? The application of SNA within academia has a long history, but its use within other fields is just beginning. The transition of the use of SNA from a more academic and theoretical focus to a more practical application means that the challenges of learning and understanding the methodology are at an innovative and potentially labor-intensive stage. Including the application of SNA to evaluation requires a risk taker, typical of first innovators. But there are currently examples of applications that can be adapted to evaluation practice, and because SNA can range from the simple to the complex in terms of theory alignment and measures used, the opportunities for implementing SNA within an evaluation design are broad.

In Chapter Four, Kochan and Teddlie used SNA to highlight how faculty characteristics affected communication patterns. Organizational division or unity based on the characteristics of members of the organization is not unique to schools. In Chapter Six, Birk illustrated the use of SNA for understanding the capacity of an organization to carry out its goals. This type of application is not unique to scientific communities. Any organization or program that has specific activities, events, or projects that require specific expertise to implement faces the same questions.

How can evaluators determine if SNA is right for their evaluation practice? We offer four suggestions. First, investigate the literature on SNA. This volume presents only a glimpse into SNA methodology and application and is not intended as an instructional manual, but rather as a gentle introduction to this field.

Second, explore the existing evaluation questions and goals as an evaluation design is developed. Evaluators should look for those goals or questions that indicate relationships. For example, an evaluation may include data collection to determine the extent of collaboration among team members. By including a question that asks about those whom individuals collaborate with and the frequency of that collaboration, attribute data can be evaluated within the context of how collaboration takes place. This question is different from knowing who should be collaborating with whom based on assignments or team memberships. In addition, there are numerous measures for indicating a relationship, for example, the number and type of e-mail or discussion group messages, as well as survey data.

If SNA is something that suits your current area of practice, then our third suggestion is to start with a few measures and work with an expert to develop the initial data collection instruments and analysis. The value of adding expertise by far surpasses the cost of the learning curve in terms of data collection development, choice of measures, theory construction and alignment, and data analysis and interpretation.

Our final suggestion is to incorporate the time for feedback with the client within the evaluation design. The need for feedback is critical, as interpreting a network and the importance of specific characteristics of a network is not like calculating a mean and standard deviation or summarizing qualitative statements. SNA does provide specific findings; however, the importance of specific network information is relative to specific clients and the questions and insights they have about their networks. When clients are presented with the analysis and interpretation for the first time, there is a clear realization moment when what they see in data format and what is implicit in their minds begins to come together. This clarification and discussion often lead to the second round or iteration of analysis that clarifies and extends the initial findings. For example, in Chapter Seven, Durland's analysis of the membership of the cliques led to a more through understanding of how the two teams were structured.

The interpretation of SNA data and sociograms is not a linear process. Rather, it is much like the systems it explores: complex and systemic, with the ability to explore the individual, groups, and the complete network. In this volume, we have presented only the most basic of measures and with minimum analysis for greater understanding.

SNA is about relationships, and relationships are at the core of organizations. Sociograms and network analysis data are important organizational tools because they can provide a framework for clarifying other data within the context of communication capacity. Sociograms provide a picture of the general pattern of communication or relationship studied, but this general pattern should be evaluated within the context of the major questions that are being asked and other relevant data. Usually no single characteristic is more critical than any other. Social network data, sociogram mapping, and other data fit together to tell a total story about a network.

SNA has potential applications within evaluation that go beyond this volume. Areas of future research could include the availability and spread of leadership throughout a network, the overall level of communication within a network, the identification of opportunities and constraints within a network, network power and influence, team and network performance, personnel evaluation, the ability to adapt to organizational change, potential for and spread of innovations, assessment of communities of practice, and program integration.

We hope that this volume provides a basic understanding of SNA to evaluators and sparks continued interest and use of this methodology within evaluation practice. Although this volume is not a handbook on how to conduct SNA, the references listed in "Additional Resources" provide more in-depth information. We look forward to future publications on SNA's use and utility within evaluation.

MARYANN M. DURLAND *is an independent consultant specializing in evaluation and in the applications of social network analysis.*

KIMBERLY A. FREDERICKS *is assistant professor of public administration and policy in the Department of Political Science, Indiana State University.*

Additional Resources

Software Applications

INSNA (International Network for Social Network Analysis). Links to network analysis software packages. http://www.insna.org/INSNA/soft_inf.html

UCINET6 and NetDraw. Network Analysis program with NetDraw, a visualization package. http://www.analytictech.com

KRACKPLOT. Network visualization. http://www.analytictech.com

PAJEK. Package for large network analysis. http://vlado.fmf.uni-lj.si/pub/networks/pajek

Netminer. Network analysis and visualization program. http://www.netminer.com/NetMiner/home_01.jsp

Books

Barabasi, A. L. *Linked: How Everything Is Connected to Everything Else and What It Means for Business, Science, and Everyday Life.* New York: Penguin, 2002.

Burt, R. S., and Minor, M. *Applied Network Analysis: A Methodological Introduction.* Thousand Oaks, Calif.: Sage, 1983.

Forse, M., and Degenne, A. *Introducing Social Networks.* Thousand Oaks, Calif.: Sage, 1999.

Freeman, L. C., White, D. R., and Romney, A. K. *Research Methods in Social Network Analysis.* Fairfax, Va.: George Mason University Press, 1989.

Hannemann, R. A. *Introduction to Social Network Methods.* Online textbook. http://wizard.ucr.edu/~rhannema/networks/text/textindex.html

Kilduff, M., and Tsai, W. *Social Networks and Organizations.* Thousand Oaks, Calif.: Sage, 2003.

Knoke, D., and Kuklinski, J. *Network Analysis.* Thousand Oaks, Calif.: Sage, 1982.

Monge, P. R., and Contractor, N. S. *Theories of Communication Networks.* London: Oxford University Press, 2003.

Scott, J. *Social Network Analysis.* Thousand Oaks, Calif.: Sage, 1992.

Valente, T. *Network Models of the Diffusion of Innovations.* Cresskill, N.J.: Hampton Press, 1995.

Wasserman, S., and Faust, K. *Social Network Analysis*. Cambridge: Cambridge University Press, 1994.

Wellman, B., and Berkowitz, S. D. *Social Structures: A Network Approach*. Cambridge: Cambridge University Press, 1988.

Journals

Social Networks. http://eclectic.ss.uci.edu/~socnets/snjhome.html

CONNECTIONS. http://www.analytictech.com/connections

Journal of Social Structure. http://www.heinz.cmu.edu/project/INSNA/joss/index1.html

INDEX

Back Issue/Subscription Order Form

Copy or detach and send to:
Jossey-Bass, A Wiley Imprint, 989 Market Street, San Francisco CA 94103-1741

Call or fax toll-free: Phone 888-378-2537 6:30AM – 3PM PST; Fax 888-481-2665

Back Issues: Please send me the following issues at $27 each
(Important: please include series initials and issue number, such as EV101.)

_____

_____

_____

$ _____   Total for single issues

$ _____   SHIPPING CHARGES: SURFACE   Domestic   Canadian
                                    First Item $5.00 $6.00
                                    Each Add'l Item $3.00 $1.50
                     For next-day and second-day delivery rates, call the number listed above.

Subscriptions: Please __start __renew my subscription to *New Directions for Evaluation*
for the year 2 _____ at the following rate:

U.S.   __Individual $80   __Institutional $185
Canada   __Individual $80   __Institutional $225
All Others   __Individual $104   __Institutional $259

**For more information about online subscriptions visit
www.interscience.wiley.com**

$ _____   Total single issues and subscriptions (Add appropriate sales tax
for your state for single issue orders. No sales tax for U.S.
subscriptions. Canadian residents, add GST for subscriptions and
single issues.)

__Payment enclosed (U.S. check or money order only)
__VISA __MC __AmEx #_____ Exp. Date _____

Signature _____ Day Phone _____

__ Bill Me (U.S. institutional orders only. Purchase order required.)

Purchase order # _____
Federal Tax ID13559302   **GST 89102 8052**

Name _____
Address _____

_____
Phone _____ E-mail _____

For more information about Jossey-Bass, visit our Web site at **www.josseybass.com**

OTHER TITLES AVAILABLE IN THE
NEW DIRECTIONS FOR EVALUATION SERIES
Jean A. King, Editor-in-Chief

**NEW DIRECTIONS FOR EVALUATION
IS NOW AVAILABLE ONLINE AT WILEY INTERSCIENCE**

What is Wiley InterScience?

Wiley InterScience is the dynamic online content service from John Wiley & Sons delivering the full text of over 300 leading scientific, technical, medical, and professional journals, plus major reference works, the acclaimed Current Protocols laboratory manuals, and even the full text of select Wiley print books online.

What are some special features of Wiley InterScience?

Wiley Interscience Alerts is a service that delivers table of contents via e-mail for any journal available on Wiley InterScience as soon as a new issue is published online.
Early View is Wiley's exclusive service presenting individual articles online as soon as they are ready, even before the release of the compiled print issue. These articles are complete, peer-reviewed, and citable.
CrossRef is the innovative multi-publisher reference linking system enabling readers to move seamlessly from a reference in a journal article to the cited publication, typically located on a different server and published by a different publisher.

How can I access Wiley InterScience?

Visit http://www.interscience.wiley.com.

Guest Users can browse Wiley InterScience for unrestricted access to journal Tables of Contents and Article Abstracts, or use the powerful search engine.
Registered Users are provided with a *Personal Home Page* to store and manage customized alerts, searches, and links to favorite journals and articles. Additionally, Registered Users can view free Online Sample Issues and preview selected material from major reference works.
Licensed Customers are entitled to access full-text journal articles in PDF, with select journals also offering full-text HTML.

How do I become an Authorized User?

Authorized Users are individuals authorized by a paying Customer to have access to the journals in Wiley InterScience. For example, a University that subscribes to Wiley journals is considered to be the Customer. Faculty, staff and students authorized by the University to have access to those journals in Wiley InterScience are Authorized Users. Users should contact their Library for information on which Wiley journals they have access to in Wiley InterScience.

ASK YOUR INSTITUTION ABOUT WILEY INTERSCIENCE TODAY!